5-MINUTE MINDFULNESS

100 Effortless Mindfulness Tips for Abundant Happiness and Inner Peace

By Karen Gray

"Do not dwell in the past, do not dream of the future,
concentrate the mind on the present moment."

- Buddha

TABLE OF CONTENTS

INTRODUCTION

Unconscious living isn't a term that many of us will have heard, but unfortunately, it's the way a lot of us live our lives. Thinking about the future, worrying about the past, going through the day on autopilot, never actually living in the present moment. You can't control what hasn't happened yet or what has already passed, but you can enjoy the beauty of right now. If you look hard enough, it is always there.

Why are we trapped in unconscious living?

Take a moment to think about your day, about how you currently live; notice how much of it is actually this unconscious living. You wake up and immediately begin to think about everything you need to do that day – you brush your teeth while thinking about work; at work, you're constantly worried about how well that presentation just went or if you'll be able to catch up with things you're behind on. Even after you get home, you begin thinking over your day, eating while worrying about what went wrong. There's not even any escape when you go to bed, because that seems to be the time issues from years ago will crop up, giving you plenty to stress over and stop you going to sleep.

Constant access to media devices doesn't help with this. We are always "available" to be contacted via messaging and email, which makes it impossible to switch off. There is always a very rapid way to get onto our social media accounts, and a never-ending scrolling feature, which ensures we don't even know how much time we're spending on these sites, and an endless stream of notifications to keep us distracted from the present moment.

The issue is, there is always a lot to worry about, and it's very easy to get caught up in that, but when you really think about it, worrying doesn't change anything. It doesn't alter the past or make the future better, so this natural cycle we have all gotten stuck in isn't helpful at all.

Is living this way useful?

It has become useful over time because it allows us to do many things at once. Our brains are amazing things that can multitask amazingly. We can think and worry about many different things at once, which might seem like it makes us more productive – but actually, the opposite is true. Our brains have become loud and irritable.

Why is it an issue, and what does it cause?

Living unconsciously is an issue because it's affecting our health. We are more stressed and prone to anxiety and depression. More likely to turn to comfort food, eating it without realizing that we're full; more likely to engage in activities that aren't good for us. By putting on the brakes, even for a mere five minutes every day, we can start to live a quieter, simpler, and healthier life.

Has it always been a problem?

Ancient people might have had different issues from us. They were more focused on survival, food, shelter, whereas, our worries are less practical but still just as stressful. The opinions of others, social media, work issues. The effects this stress has on our bodies is still the same. It needs to be stopped.

Our brains might have evolved a lot, growing three times in size, which makes our abilities and needs different, but our desire for inner peace and our need for calm and quiet in our minds still exists. This is still very necessary.

What can we do about it?

That is where the practice of mindfulness comes in. Recommended by many medical professionals, it's recognized as one of the best ways to calm the mind and improve mental, spiritual, and physical health. It will connect you with your inner self and assist you in living the life you have always wanted to, moving you away from this unhealthy unconscious living.

Life is so busy, even for children, who can also benefit from this meditation practice, it's easy to get trapped in this vicious cycle, but there are many reasons why we need to get out of it.

This book will give you the most extensive list of new and exciting methods for trying mindfulness in a way that you can make work. By introducing this new practice into your life for the very achievable and engaging goal of five minutes at a time, for at least thirty days, it will become something manageable, rather than another stress to add to your 'to do' list.

So, read on to find the best way to build a mindfulness habit, anchoring yourself for just five short minutes, to enjoy inner peace and happiness. Find practical tools that can fit in with your life to become a more mindful person. Enjoy!

WHAT IS MINDFULNESS?

Mindfulness is the practice of living in the present moment, which sounds far easier than it actually is. When you begin to notice these things, you'll see how it's actually become normal for us to live unconsciously, moving through life on autopilot. We spend so much time worrying about the past and panicking about the future, about what we need to do when we get home or how big our work 'to do' list is. While we're doing all of this thinking, living in another time, we're missing what's happening right now.

Living in the 'right now,' even if only for a short while, is what mindfulness wants to help you achieve.

There are many **physical and psychological benefits to mindfulness**, including:

- *General well-being* – studies (at have shown a dramatic improvement in life satisfaction and happiness, leading to a healthier life, by using mindfulness(www.sciencedirect.com/science/article/pii/S0272735 815000197)

- *Physical health* – scientists have found that the reduction in stress and the cortisol chemical in the body leads to a much healthier body overall. It's now part of most healthcare plans for people with chronic long-term conditions (www.sciencedirect.com/science/article/pii/S0022399903005737)

- *Mental health* – research has also determined significant improvements for people who live with chronic mental conditions such as anxiety and depression (www.sciencedirect.com/science/article/pii/S027273581100081X)

Other benefits include help with heart issues, reduction in chronic pain, lower blood pressure, better sleep, and an alleviation of gastrointestinal difficulties.

So, what exactly is mindfulness?

As previously stated, it is living in the present moment, without thoughts constantly bombarding you, dragging you away from what's happening right now. It's being aware of this moment without thinking about the past and the future. It's having a detached awareness of life right now.

Mindful awareness is achieved in various ways. When people hear the word *'mindfulness,'* they often associate it with meditation, and while it can be achieved in that way, there are a number of ways in which you can practice it. It's a very personal thing, and it's up to you to find a way that works best for you and fits into your lifestyle – because if it doesn't do that, then you're unlikely to keep it up.

10 STEPS TO BUILDING A MINDFULNESS HABIT

"The real meditation is how you live your life."
– Jon Kabat-Zinn

Mindfulness is a habit, or it can be. When the practice becomes a habit, it will be something that you do every single day without even having to think about it. This way, you will end up getting the benefits from it, without having to worry too much about it.

Still need convincing? Here are **ten reasons why you should give it a try**, with scientific support so you can see how research proves this useful:

1. It increases immune function, helping your body to fight and prevent illness – *Mindful Meditation Can Produce Alterations for Immune System and Brain Function.*

2. It has been proven to raise your serotonin levels and happiness – *Build Your Life with an Open Heart: Loving-Kindness Mindful Meditation*

Creates Positive Emotions, Increases Emotional Resources (psycnet.apa.org/ record/2008-14857-004).

3. Mindfulness also assists you in improving your self-control and regulating your emotions — *Training in Compassion Cultivation: Effects on Emotion Regulation, Affect, and Mindfulness (Randomized, Controlled Trial).*

4. The meditation practice boosts cortical thickness for regions of the brain affecting attention span — *Modified Cortical Thickness After Mindful Meditation Practice (www.ncbi.nlm.nih.gov/pmc/articles/PMC1361 002/)*

5. It improves your memory and therefore makes you a more productive person — *Mental Training Evidence Shows Mindfulness Meditation Can Improve Cognition (www.sciencedirect.com/science/article/ pii/S1053810010000681).*

6. It decreases inflammation at the cellular level — *Comparing Efforts for Modulating Neurogenic Inflammation with Mindful Reduction of Stress (www.sciencedirect.com/science/article/pii/S0889159112004758).*

7. Mindfulness enhances compassion and emotional intelligence — *A Randomized, Controlled Trial in Enhancing Emotional Intelligence Based on Training in Mindful Cultivation of Compassion.*

8. It improves introspection, allowing you to see yourself and the situations that you find yourself in a much clearer way — *Clarifying Connection Between Physiology and Emotional Experience Using Mindfulness (www.ocf.berkeley.edu/~agyurak/Szeatal_E_2010.pdf)*

9. It increases the brain's grey matter, which includes areas that affect self-control, decision-making, speech, muscle control, memory, emotion, and our range of senses — *Tracing How Long-Term Mindful Meditation Correlates to Volume Changes in Grey Matter and the Hippocampus (www.sciencedirect.com/science/article/pii/S1053811909000 044).*

10. It makes it much easier to multitask — *The Effects of Mindful Meditation on Multitasking Performance (dl.acm.org/citation.cfm?id=19798 62)*

So, how do you develop this into a habit?

Adding more into your schedule, which I'm sure is already very busy, probably isn't going to feel like something that's achievable, but there are many ways that you can make it happen. When building this new habit becomes a priority, there are things you can do to ensure it sticks.

"Habits are behaviors which are performed automatically because they have been performed frequently in the past. This repetition creates a mental association between the situation (cue) and action (behavior) which means that when the cue is encountered the behavior is performed automatically. Automaticity has a number of components, one of which is lack of thought." – according to *routineexcellence.com/psychology-of-habits-form-habits-make-stick/*

As you can see from this sentence, there are three parts to this. The *cue*, the *action*, and the *reward*. The cue is the thing that reminds you to take part in the habit – in this case, the mindfulness habit. That can be an alarm on your phone at the same time every day, which reminds you to do your five minutes, set for a time that you know will work best, or a certain event that reminds you it's time. Then there's the action, the mindfulness practice. The next chapter of this book will give you one hundred examples of practices that you can try, which will be followed by part three, the reward.

The feeling that you will get after performing mindfulness and living in the moment will be reward enough. The calm and inner peace you'll experience will be a real buzz, but while you are trying to turn this into a habit, you can introduce another reward to thank yourself for taking this time for yourself. A treat, a log in a journal, ticking it off a list, read a page of your favorite book – whatever makes you feel good, do that afterwards.

While you are planning your habit, it can help to **consider the following factors**:

- **Time** – what time of day will suit you every day? When can you take five minutes for yourself? When you wake up, before you go to sleep, after work? Make sure it's realistic – that when your phone alarm goes off, you will be able to do it right away. You won't put it off, then forget.

- **Space** – it can be really nice to have a calm, peaceful place to do your mindfulness. Not a messy room or one that you associate with chaos. It needs to be somewhere that relaxes you, that you will be able to switch off without thinking too much about what you need to do.

- **Intention** – this is actually one of the most important things. The intention to find calm and to make time. If you don't have this, then the habit will never happen.

- **Consistency** – this is something that you want to do every single day, at least for the first thirty days, while you examine the benefits that mindfulness can have for you, and to help build the habit. That's why the same time every day is helpful.

- **Social support** – everyone in your life, especially in your home, if that's where you intend to perform the mindfulness, needs to be aware what you're doing so they will give you the space to take those five minutes to yourself.

- **Log** – it can be really helpful to keep a record of the first thirty days to see the effect that it's having on you. Write down your mood, feelings, and thoughts before, then afterwards as well. This will remind you why stepping out of autopilot and taking a powerful pause is the best thing for you.

Here is a list of **ten practical steps to creating this mindfulness habit** if you're still struggling:

1. *Know your reasons* – list why you feel like you need inner peace, then you can refer back to it whenever you aren't in the mood or it feels hard. There is something that you wish to achieve, and it can be helpful to recall that.

2. *Start small* – begin with some of the five-minute exercises. Then if you want to progress and you think you might benefit from a longer mindfulness moment, you can make that happen.

3. *Find a trigger* – if the phone alarm doesn't work, then tie it to something that you're already doing every single day – taking a shower or eating breakfast. Combine it to make it easier.

4. *Make a comfortable space* – ensure that where you meditate is

somewhere that feels comfortable and calms you.

5. *Choose your method* – some people like to combine mindfulness with an activity; other people like to close their eyes to block the rest of the world out.

6. *Make it fun* – if you enjoy something, you are more likely to do it, so make it a pleasurable experience. Light a candle that you like the smell of, or use music. Make it lovely.

7. *Hold yourself accountable* – a way to make sure that you follow through on the habit is to do it with someone else. If that isn't possible, find another way to make sure that you keep it up for the thirty days.

8. *Don't make excuses* – five minutes isn't much time. Everyone can find five minutes somewhere, especially when it's an activity that can be combined with something else. So make sure that you do it every single day.

9. *Track your progress* – this is why the journal is a good idea, but if that's too much like hard work, use a chart or an app to track your progress.

10. Then there is the *reward* – finding something to make yourself even happier will assist you in sticking to it.

Just remember, this doesn't have to be something very complicated, something you need to remember and carve out time for. It can be difficult to find even five minutes when your days get hectic. If that's the case for you, then you can include it with activities you are already doing every single day, making it part of what you already have to do – shower, eat, walk. This book will give you plenty of exercises to combine with your current lifestyle, making it even easier to build this habit.

But, of course, before you can start building this habit, you need to practice the exercises, so read on for one hundred ways to get yourself started. By using a selection of the hundred exercises for the next thirty days to work out what suits you and your lifestyle, you will begin carving out five minutes for yourself every single day – which you can do no matter how busy you are. Once you get this time to yourself and work out which exercises benefit you the most, you can move forward in a mindful way tailored to you and your individual needs – turning thirty days into a positive lifelong habit.

10 LITTLE-KNOWN MINDFULNESS FACTS

For even more reassurance that mindfulness has transformative benefits, here are **ten facts that most people don't know**:

1. Celebrities love mindfulness. A popular fan is the very successful Richard Branson. He says that it's *"one way that many entrepreneurs choose to combat the toll wrought by round-the-clock emails, long working hours and other aspects of our accelerate business culture."* (*www.virgin.com/entrepreneur/three-reasons-we-should-all-practise-mindfulness*)

2. Online searches for the term 'mindfulness' have increased 67% in the last five years.

3. Our mind can process 126 pieces of information every second, but we spend most of our time using our brains to ignore what's around us right now.

4. Mindfulness is not a religious concept, but it has been practiced by Buddhists for more than 2,500 years.

5. The Google company has introduced policies that encourage teams and offices to practice mindfulness, especially in meetings. Additionally, over thirty-five offices provide time for their employees to practice mindfulness daily, and five locations provide the time for retreats that last an entire day.

6. Despite the long-standing belief that the brain could not generate new cells, research into practicing mindfulness regularly has proved this wrong. The production of new cells helps people alleviate stress and live a more peaceful life.

7. Practicing mindfulness over time has the power to literally alter your brain's wiring. Enhancing neuroplasticity, regular practice will make the emotional, physical, and psychological benefits of

mindfulness permanent.

8. According to Balance Media (*balance.media/mindfulness-facts/*), the following are the most mindful cities in the world:

   - Aarhus, Denmark
   - Bergen, Norway
   - Lucerne, Switzerland
   - Reykjavik, Iceland
   - Turku, Finland

9. The brain cannot sustain regular concentration for an extended period of time. It works best when focus is applied for around ninety minutes and is most effective when short breaks are taken from the work regularly.

10. The research into mindfulness is growing all the time, as shown by this diagram:

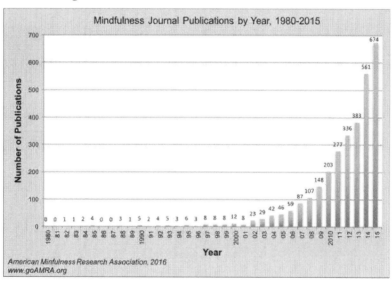

100 PROVEN TIPS
FOR PRACTICING
MINDFULNESS TODAY

"Surrender to what is. Let go of what was. Have faith in what will be."
– Sonia Ricotti

This chapter will give you one hundred mindfulness tips and exercises to get you started with living a calmer life by being in tune with the present. This will bring you abundant happiness and inner peace. Try as many or as few as you like, if you don't think that they will suit you, but choose some to do over the next thirty days. You can even try a different one every single day, to see how it makes you feel.

Keeping a record of this will help you to remember what works best for you, but, of course, this is your journey, feel free to do whatever feels right to you.

Mindfulness Anchoring Techniques

1. MINDFUL BREATHING

Mindful breathing is something that can be done any time of day, no matter what you're doing, and can be done for as long as you require. Breathing is something that we do all the time – it's what we do to keep us alive – so it's something that we always have with us. You can also do it without anyone knowing, so it's always possible.

It's great for **creating a little head space for yourself**, to calm down stressful situations or moments where emotions flare, or just for a second of peace:

- Find a calm place to get you started. If you're just starting mindfulness practices, it's easier when you have a designated space.

- Settle yourself into a comfortable position. You don't want to have to keep moving around because you don't feel right.

- Set a timer for five minutes. Then it's time to begin.

- This can be something done with your eyes open or closed, but if they're open, have a soft focus. Don't look at anything in particular.

- Then it's time to breathe. Inhale through your nose; exhale through your mouth. Deep breaths at first to really experience the sensation of the air travelling through your body before returning to your normal pattern of breathing.

- Notice the sensations, how the air feels in your body, how your stomach expands and falls, your chest rises with each breath.

- If your mind wanders, every time you notice it, bring your focus back to your breath and your body. This isn't something to punish yourself over. Everyone does it. The mind is used to wandering. Just notice it and return to your breath. Remember that there isn't anything else that you need to be doing during this time. It's a moment for you to just be.

- Once the five minutes is over, slowly open your eyes or return to the room and notice how differently you feel now.

2. MINDFUL OBSERVATION

Mindful observation is noticing your direct sensory experience. What you can see, hear, feel, smell, and taste. We experience the world around us all the time without really noticing it, so **this exercise is just taking five minutes to just really experience it all**.

This exercise is a wonderful one to do outside in nature, where the world is a beautiful place, but if that isn't possible, then find somewhere that makes you feel happy and calm:

- The best way to start this exercise is with mindful breathing to ground yourself. Focus on your breath for a while, until your thoughts have stopped racing. If it helps to close your eyes, you can for some of this exercise. Can you taste anything on your breath while you're doing this?

- Feel your body first. Where you are sitting or standing, what your body is touching. Notice these things without labelling them with judgement. Don't worry about if you do or don't like a sensation, just experience it.

- Let the sounds around you fall on your ears, again, without judgement. You don't even need to worry about working out what the sounds are.

- Then, if your eyes are closed, it's time to softly and gently open your eyes and just see what's in your direct line of vision.

- Experience all these things at once for the rest of the five minutes, really connecting and just being where you are.

3. MINDFUL AWARENESS

Mindful awareness is not about blocking out thoughts, positive or negative, but instead, being aware of them and letting them go. Negativity isn't something that we can completely exist without; it happens without our control. And the more that we try to get rid of it, the worse it will rear its ugly head. The best thing that you can do is just notice these thoughts, but then let them slide away without getting too stuck on them. When we live unconsciously, we can get tangled up in these thoughts without even realizing it. The practice of mindful awareness is a way to get out of this bad habit.

Here is a great **five-minute exercise** to practice this:

- Sit upright in a relaxed position and close your eyes.

- Take a few deep breaths while focusing on the sensations in your body. How are you are feeling physically, emotionally, mentally? Just observe this.

- As you breathe in, notice the sensation of the breath in your nostrils.

- Notice everything in your body, not just the position of it. Are you hot or cold? Achy anywhere? Is there any pressure? Simply observe this. Don't get caught up in it.

- If, at any point, the mind wanders, just see where it wandered to. Then guide your mind back to focusing on the sensations of your breath. How it feels going in your nose and coming out your mouth. Concentrate only on that for a while.

- Include sounds in your awareness. What can you hear inside the room, and outside too. Allow them to fall on your ears without worrying too much or getting caught up in what sounds are and what they mean.

- Any thoughts that pop into your brain, allow them to simply slide away. Pass by like clouds floating through the sky. Bring awareness to the thoughts themselves. Even the thought, *"I don't know what I'm doing,"* is a thought.

- Just like with sounds, we can also notice our thoughts, as if we were sitting in a dark movie theatre, noticing the dialogue and the images come and go on the screen. So, beginning now, bring awareness to the thoughts themselves. Notice an opening up, being aware.

- Breathe in and breathe out, and as we gently come back to the breath, notice how the whole body expands on an inhalation, contracts on an exhalation. We can genuinely thank ourselves for taking this time out of our day just to engage in this practice for our health and well-being.

4. MINDFUL IMMERSION

Mindful immersion is really immersing yourself in something for five minutes. Find an activity that you enjoy most of all and give everything of yourself to it to ensure that you get the absolute most out of it. It can be tai chi or yoga, or even showering. Something that you can give your **undivided attention to for five minutes**:

- Start with some mindful breathing, center yourself, anchor to where you are right now in this moment. Close your eyes and do some deep breaths if this helps you. Feel the breath circling through your body.

- Then start the activity. As you do, use your five senses. Can you smell or taste anything? Especially if the activity you're taking part in is cooking or something like that. What can you see and hear? How does your body feel? Really notice all of these things and think about them without judgement.

- If your mind wanders, just note that it has and bring it back to your activity, focusing only on that for five minutes.

5. GAME OF FOUR SQUARE

The game of four square is another way to look at how our minds wander off and drift when we're living on autopilot. The blue circle in the middle of the square is the present moment, where we want to be right now. But, often, our mind is living in the past – either in a positive way (*nostalgia*) or in a negative way (*regret*) – or in the future, in *fantasy* or *fear*.

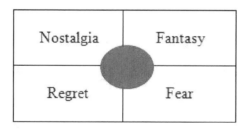

Here is a great way you can **get past all of these thoughts** and you can just **anchor yourself to the present**:

- 1 deep breath
- 2 scents I enjoy or can smell
- 3 objects I enjoy the feeling of or can touch
- 4 sounds I enjoy or can hear
- 5 objects I enjoy seeing or can see

Every time you notice your mind getting distracted by the past or the future, try this quick exercise to bring you back again.

6. FIVE SENSES

Using your five senses is a great way to anchor yourself and to bring yourself into the present moment, particularly at a time of stress or high emotion when meditating feels impossible. What you can see, hear, and touch is a perfect way to focus on the right now rather than thoughts. Thoughts and emotions might crop up when doing this exercise, but that's okay. Don't use it as a way to punish yourself. Just observe the thoughts, notice them, then return to the senses.

Here is **a five senses exercise** for that:

- Stand or sit in a comfortable position, where your feet are planted flat on the ground and your arms and hands are at rest. Begin with mindful breathing.

- Focus on every one of your senses. Apply awareness to each one separately. The order presented below isn't a requirement, you can focus on each on in the order you prefer.

- *Hear*: Focus on all the sounds around you, distant and nearby. Don't place judgement on them, simply notice them.

- *Smell*: Close your eyes, then inhale deeply through your nose. Simply notice the smells all around you. Don't place judgement on them, simply notice them.

- *See*: Open your eyes and look around yourself. Place your awareness on colors, textures, and shapes you may not notice otherwise.

- *Taste*: Run your tongue over your teeth and between your lips. What can you taste? Even if it's nothing, that's okay. Just notice this without judgement.

- *Touch*: Observe how your body is resting or standing in the space you've chosen. Focus on this sensation. For example, the chair you are sitting on, the temperature of the air around you, or how your clothes feel against your skin.

- After you have performed focus for each sense, observe how your body feels. How is this new awareness making you feel? If you are experiencing a positive change, make the intention to carry this awareness with you and practice it whenever you feel stress or tension.

7. DO NOTHING

The aim of mindfulness is to help you learn to relax, which can be achieved by taking five minutes to just do nothing. In our busy lives, with a never-ending 'to do' list, we very rarely do nothing. Our brains even less so. When we're sitting down for a moment for a coffee, our brain is still off somewhere else, working at a million miles an hour.

You deserve five minutes to yourself, to just be and to just do nothing, and during that time, there is nothing else that you need to think of at all. Nothing you need to worry about or do. That is time carved out for just you. Having this time will actually make you more productive in the long run, so take some time to switch your brain off.

Here is **a do nothing meditation** for you:

- Simply, the instruction would be to sit down, comfortably, and do nothing.

- Should you require more instruction than that, the meditation can be broken down into steps. Because you will be doing something, technically, paying attention.

- Allow your mind to conjure thoughts, feelings, and emotions. You don't even have to let them pass by. Allow the distraction. Noticing how you think and realize that when you think you are doing something; you are being active. Then, you realize that letting go of those thoughts is an active choice, as well.

- If it starts to feel like your mind is getting caught up in thoughts, emotions, trying to meditate, and struggling to clear your mind, let those thoughts float away.

- Notice how your body feels. Are you sensing a constriction or tension in your muscles or your mind? Let this sensation float away, too.

- Maintain that sense of doing nothing, simply relaxing.

- Practice this meditation for as much time as you prefer. Maintain clear awareness and stop when you are too distracted or feeling fatigue.

8. MINDFUL CHECK-IN

Checking in with yourself sporadically, or even to a timer, every so often throughout the day is a good way to keep yourself aware of the present moment for longer. After practicing a moment of mindfulness, it sticks with you for a while, causing more of your day to be lived within the present, so having lots of check-ins will assist you with this.

Here is **a brief mindful check-in** to try:

- Become aware of your experience right now.

- What sensations in the body do you feel? Scan your body starting at the soles of your feet all the way to the crown of your head.

- You may sense tightness or tension in areas of the body or notice your stomach rumbling because it's close to lunchtime. You may become aware that you feel chilly or warm. Maybe you feel tired.

- What thoughts are going through your mind? Try to acknowledge the nature or content of thoughts without getting caught up in them. For example, if you are thinking about an upcoming meeting or appointment, what feelings are present? You don't need to do anything about them, just recognize that you feel worried, frustrated, etc.

- Narrow your attention to the breath. Focus on the physical sensations of breathing. For example, feel the breath in the abdomen as it expands and releases. Focus on your breath as it moves in and out; use your breath as an anchor to the present.

- Expand your awareness. Let your attention expand to become aware of the body as a whole, sitting/standing and breathing, from the top of your head to the tips of your toes.

- Feel where the body meets the chair or floor.

- And then expand out even further to include the temperature of the room and the space around you. What sounds do you hear? What do you see?

9. COUNT YOUR BREATHS

If you find yourself struggling with the mindful breaths, no matter what exercise you try, if you're having issues with your mind always wandering off and you can't seem to get focused, you can always count your breaths as a way of keeping your brain where it needs to be.

Don't worry too much about the counting; it's important not to get caught up in it, because that isn't the point of the meditation. It's just a way to anchor yourself, so don't count higher than ten, and if you forget where you are, don't worry about it. Just start again. Here are **some tips to help you with this**:

- Sit in a comfortable position and start breathing deeply, then pause.
- Count one after you exhale. Then, inhale again, pause, and count two after you exhale.
- Count after each exhale like that until you get to ten.
- After you reach ten, start to count each exhale going backward. Start with nine, until you get back to one.
- If a thought should interrupt your counting, and you forget which number you were on, start over again from one.
- Try to get up to ten and back to one without any interruptions.

10. ANCHORING

For most of these mindfulness exercises, your breath is your anchor. That's what you focus on to bring you into the present moment, and that's where you bring yourself back to if you find your mind drifting. But if that doesn't work for you, there are other things you can try to anchor yourself.

Here are some other things that can **bring you back to the present**:

- Other body parts – stroke your hands and anchor yourself in the sensations. Feel how your feet are planted on the floor. Use that hard sensation to keep you in place. Chew on your thumb and feel how your teeth feel on your skin.

- An item – hold something precious and meaningful to you and really feel every bit of it. Use the emotions it brings up to continually anchor yourself.

- A sound – you can have a sound playing, such as a mindfulness bell, to bring yourself back to what you want to be focusing on.

- An item of clothing – that material on your skin can keep reminding you of the present moment.

- A picture or something to look at – this might make your mind wander, but you can easily bring it back to the colors or the lines of the image.

11. FINGER BREATHING

Finger breathing is an excellent way to combine the anchors of breathing and touch and is particularly useful for those struggling to stay in the present moment, people dealing with big emotions, or even children. It's a great way to encourage that focus.

Here is **a guideline for this exercise**:

- Stare at your hand for a moment and spread the fingers wide. Observe the appearance of your hand for a few seconds before using the finger on your other hand to trace around the shape of it.

- Start at the bottom of your thumb and slide your finger up your thumb, pause at the top, and then slide your finger down the other side, breathing in as you go up, and out as you go down.

- Repeat this as you travel up and down the rest of your fingers. Once finished, you can end the practice there or start again if you need to.

5 Finger Breathing

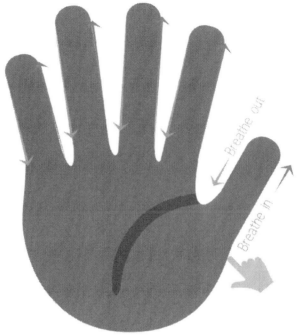

Breathe out

Breathe in

12. HANDS

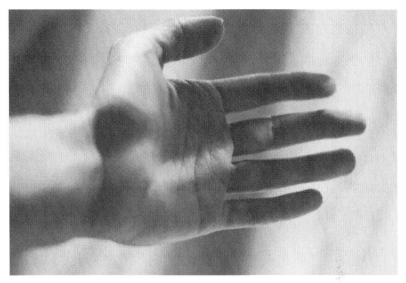

Hands are a good tool to use with mindfulness, particularly if you find it a challenge to center in on your breath. **Your hands are always there**, always attached to you, and you can **study them for five minutes or less**, until you feel grounded, even when at work or surrounded by other people:

- Start with three mindful breaths to anchor yourself, then look down at your chosen hand.

- Start with the back of your hand, noticing any freckles or imperfections, without judgements. Notice any bumps or lines. Move your hand around to see how it looks different as you do.

- Stroke your hand and notice the sensations. How does it make you feel?

- Then turn the hand over and study your palm. What marks are there? What lines? Again, move your hand around and notice any changes.

- Keep this up for five minutes, or however long you have chosen, until you feel grounded.

13. STOP

Stopping is a big part of mindfulness, pausing and taking a moment for yourself. This exercise uses an acronym to help you with your mindfulness. By thinking of the word STOP, you should be able to **remember what you need to do:**

- **Stillness**. Establish a connection to your environment and the earth. Anchor yourself in the present moment and how you feel right now. Are there any thoughts or emotions that crop up? Simply observe them and let them slide by.

- **Thoughtful**. Give yourself a mindful check-in. Acknowledge the sensations within your body, and use mindful breathing to inhale peace and exhale any of unpleasant feelings.

- **Observation**. Open your eyes. Focus on your immediate environment. Shift your awareness toward something that is pleasant. Be intentional and feel gratitude for that pleasantness. Carry gratitude and appreciation with you to give you some joy.

- **Potential**. Consider what your next step is from here, all that is possible. Where do you go from here? Don't worry about everything that you need to do for the rest of the day, simply consider your very next step.

14. BREATHING COLORS

We have talked about color before and how to use it for mindfulness, but the breathing colors exercise below is a little different. It's not finding colors, but **about looking inward instead**:

- Sit comfortably and close your eyes, anchoring yourself with a few mindful breaths.
- Imagine you are surrounded by the relaxing color. No longer is the air clear; it is the relaxing color.
- You can still make out shapes, but your world is now a different color.
- Imagine that, as you breathe in, you breathe in this color too.
- See the color filling up your lungs.
- Imagine, as you breathe out, that your breath is the color of stress.
- See the stress color mix into the relaxing color around you. Watch the stress color slowly disappear.
- Breath in your relaxing color.
- Breath out the stress color.

15. HEARTBEATS

Your heartbeat is a natural rhythm that you can use to focus on, to bring you into the present moment. Meditating along with your heart rate will give you a better awareness of your body as a whole, and studies have shown that you can actually end up controlling your heart's pace, which is great for many mental and physical ailments such as asthma, autism, and trauma.

Here is a **three-minute meditation practice** for this:

- Find a comfortable sitting position.
- Use your neck or wrist to locate your pulse, and make sure to locate a pulse that is strong enough to keep your focus.
- Give yourself three quiet minutes; use a timer.
- Use this time to count your pulse, every heartbeat, as best you can.
- Log your counts.

16. SMELL THE FLOWERS

The saying 'stop and smell the roses' really applies here, but how often do you actually do it? Your sense of smell is important, and since smelling is something that you normally do passively, it's a great idea to engage and smell actively, really paying attention to what you're doing.

Below is a **wonderful mindfulness exercise for this**. It doesn't have to be done with a flower, it can be anything that smells nice, but it's a flower used as an example here:

- Stand or sit in a quiet place. Soften your gaze and focus on the flower. Notice the color, the shape and size of the flower and its parts, the petals, the stem, and the leaves.

- Now touch the flower and its parts, first, the petals, then the stem and leaves. Intentionally focus on discovering the sensations of each part. How do the petals feel? How different is that from the stem, the leaves? As you run your hand and fingers over the flower, do you hear any sounds? Use each of your senses to explore the flower and its parts.

- Now, as the title of this section suggests, bring the flower's petals up to your nose and inhale, full and deep. Do the petals brush against your skin? Focus on the natural fragrance of the petals. How does the aroma make you feel? Smell the leaves and stem. Do they have an aroma? Notice how different it is from the petals.

- Now, take a moment to mindfully reflect on the entire flower. Relax, and keep breathing mindfully, holding the flower between your fingers. You could close your eyes, and try visualizing the flower from memory. Remember the texture, the scent, the sensation of the stem and leaves between your fingers. Now, you can use this moment of exploration from memory whenever you need a mindful moment to ground or center yourself. With intention, you can carry this moment of mindful exploration and quiet with you wherever you are – for use with grounding, as an anchor, or to center your emotions if you can't literally hold a flower in your fingers.

- After forming a clear memory to recall, slowly open your eyes, take one last mindful breath, and stretch to return to your day's activities.

Mindfulness In Everyday Activities

17. MINDFUL EATING

Eating is something that we do every single day, more than once a day, but more often than not, it is something that's done in a hurry, without paying any actual attention to what we're doing. As we chew quickly, we reply to emails on our phone, we think about the rest of the day, we stress over something that's happened – none of that is helpful. We need to eat, and while we're eating, there isn't anything else that we need to do or think about during that time.

By practicing mindful eating, we also develop better eating habits. We find out more about what we actually like to eat, how eating certain foods makes us feel, and we tend to eat because our body is giving us hunger signs rather than because we only have a moment to grab lunch right now or because we're bored. It also helps us to stop eating when we're full, which **leads to a much healthier lifestyle overall**:

- Start with a bit of mindful breathing to clear the mind before starting. This will assist you in anchoring yourself to the right now and the present moment. Take a look at your plate as you breathe and take note of the colors of the food. Perhaps even consider where the food has come from.

- Then, start chewing. Eat slowly. Noticing the texture and the taste of your food as you do. How it feels in your mouth and on your tongue. As you swallow, how does it feel? Are there any sensations in your body?

- Have an awareness of everything around you before you take your next bite. What is your environment like? What do you notice? Really engage with this moment.

- Then start chewing again and repeat the cycle until you feel full.

18. MINDFUL LISTENING

More often than not, when we are supposed to be listening to other people, we aren't really listening. We are making internal judgments about what they're saying or planning what our next words will be. Sometimes, our minds drift off entirely, and we think about something else.

We aren't really engaging with the other person, which means you aren't making the most of the social or business interaction. You aren't getting the most out of it. **Listening properly improves your focus, your empathy, and your emotional intelligence**. Plus, it will make you more likeable to other people, because people like to be listened to when they talk:

- You can practice this by just listening. Close your eyes, anchor yourself with your breath, and just listen to what's going on around you. Notice the sound and tone of every noise, without passing judgement.

- You can also do this while listening to someone else. Make a plan to not judge, to not talk back, to just listen. You can ask a friend to help you with this.

- Another way to do this is to ask someone to work with you and to just speak freely for three minutes each. Don't think or plan when it's your turn to talk, just let your mind flow, and then when it's your friend's turn, just listen without interruption.

- This is a skill that gets better with practice, so keep on doing it and see the results of your more improved communication skills.

19. THE RAISIN EXERCISE

The raisin exercise is another method of eating mindfully, but in a specific way. A raisin is often used because of its unique texture and flavor. It's an exercise that goes back to early Buddhist teachings of mindfulness and is preferred for early mindfulness, when users are getting used to the new exercise.

Kabat-Zinn discusses the experience of raisin mindfulness:

"The raisin exercise dispels all previous concepts we may be harboring about meditation. It immediately places it in the realm of the ordinary, the everyday, the world you already know but are now going to know differently. Eating one raisin very, very slowly allows you to drop right into the knowing in ways that are effortless, totally natural, and entirely beyond words and thinking. Such an exercise delivers wakefulness immediately. There is in this moment only tasting."

Here is **a great way to perform this exercise**:

- Sit comfortably in a quiet room where you are least likely to be distracted.

- Use just one raisin. Hold it in your hand. Use your eyes, hands, and fingers to examine it, acting as if this is the first raisin you've ever seen. Note the aroma, color, texture, and shape.

- With intention, use each of your five senses to really explore the raisin. Allow this exploration to stimulate some memories, emotions, and thoughts. Acknowledge them, then let them float away without judgement.

- How is the raisin making you feel? Hungry? Disgusted? Nostalgic?
- Put the raisin on your tongue, move it around in your mouth. Focus on the sensation of feeling the raisin against your tongue and the roof of your mouth.
- Bite into it and notice the squishiness of it. Chew it three times carefully, noticing the sensations with every bite.
- Chew three more times and then stop.
- Consider the texture and flavor of the raisin. Does it make you feel anything?
- As you complete chewing, swallow the raisin smilingly.
- Sit quietly, breathing, aware of what you are sensing.

20. MINDFUL SEEING

Mindful seeing is a new way of seeing, by really looking at things. If you have a good imagination, this can be a good time to let your creativity run free. Use colors, various sights, and art to inspire you. This is a really good exercise to try with children, who often find a visual stimulus easier to work with than just trying to quiet the mind.

Positive Psychology (*www.positivepsychologyprogram.com*) suggests, *"This exercise only lasts a few minutes but can open up a world of discovery in an otherwise familiar place."*

The exercise that they suggest is:

- Find a window to sit at with a view.

- Look at everything there is. Instead of labeling all you can see, notice the colors and textures, the shapes and the shades.

- Try and look at the view as if it's the first time you're seeing it.

- Be observant, but not critical. Be aware, but not fixated.

- If your mind wanders, just notice what your thoughts are and bring them back to the view outside. Find something in the view to center you.

21. STEP OUT OF AUTOPILOT

This book has talked a lot about autopilot and living unconsciously, which means our brain is constantly thinking about nothing in particular, living in the future or in the past, barely noticing what's going on right now. Washing the dishes while thinking about work, walking while looking at your phone screen, lying in bed panicking about tomorrow – none of that is healthy, which is why taking five minutes a day to step out of this mode will have a good effect on you.

Most people who start to practice mindfulness, even for these five minutes a day, will soon find themselves living in a more mindful way naturally, existing with a quieter mind. Since most of our thoughts are unnecessary and unhelpful, clearing them out is a good idea.

Pick an activity that you do every single day on autopilot – the example used here will be brushing your teeth because it's something that you do in the morning, setting you up for a calmer day, and before bed, helping you to get better sleep:

- Start by putting the toothpaste on the toothbrush, and brush.
- Breathe mindfully through your nose. It helps to relax your jaw and neck.
- Focus on the bristles as they move over your gums and teeth. Notice the flavor of the toothpaste.
- Loosen your grip on the toothbrush.
- While you rinse your teeth, continue to breathe mindfully through your nose.
- Run the tip of your tongue over your clean teeth.
- Think about what your teeth help you to do, and then feel intentional gratitude for them.

22. MINDFULNESS BELL

A mindfulness bell is a specific sound that is there to remind you to take a moment of mindfulness. If you don't think you can do five minutes all in one go, then there are many apps you can use to set five bells throughout the day, to just take a minute each time.

Mindfulness bell apps include Plum Village (*plumvillage.app*), Mind Bell, and Spire.

During this minute, **you can do one of the following**:

- Mindfully breathe, count your breaths until ten, then start again. Complete this until the minute is over.

- Yawn and stretch, really feeling the sensations in your body.

- Stroke your hands and experience the sensations.

- Clench your fists and release the tension in your hands. Notice the difference between each action.

- Chose an intention for how you want to continue on until the next mindful bell and make an effort to ensure that happens.

23. COLOR CENTER

A good way to use color in mindfulness is to choose it as a trigger. We see lots of colors in our day, and by noticing these and using them to ground and center us, we will automatically begin to live a little more mindfully.

Here are **some great ideas to help you get started** with this, using traffic lights as a wonderful color source that you can use for a moment of mindfulness while waiting in traffic or trying to cross the road:

- *Red*: When you see the color red (even at a stop light), literally stop and take three breaths in and out through your nose. As you breathe through your nose, you access the parasympathetic nervous system, which naturally calms and relaxes you. Bonus points if you can breathe through the entire cycle of a red light.

- *Yellow*: When you see the color yellow, simply smile. When we smile, we release endorphins that reduce stress and help us feel better. Even faking a smile can lead to feeling happier.

- *Green*: When you see the color green, simply give gratitude. This can be as simple as being grateful that you are alive, or grateful for a loved one in your life, or grateful that you are able to embrace this moment, right here, right now. Bonus points if you want to place your hand on your heart.

24. WATCH THE WORLD GO BY

Watching the world go by can be a bit like mindful observation, but you can open your mind even more. Use all of your senses, consider everything in your body, enjoy the moment of just being. You can think about the world in a mindful way and consider your place in it. You can think about the grass, the sky, space above – as long as you're connected in a mindful way.

This great exercise talks **about using the clouds above for mindfulness**:

- Lie on your back outside, somewhere comfortable where you can stare up at the clouds.

- Gently inhale to expand your belly, and exhale to pull the belly back in. Repeat this breath, letting your body become relaxed and full of breath. After ten long breaths in and out, slowly begin to move your attention out of your belly and up into your head. Spend just a few moments noticing your breath; now spend some time noticing your thoughts. 'Noticing' means you see that something is there, but you don't have to do anything at all with it. You have the choice of what you do after you notice something, but noticing it is the first step before choosing.

- Take some time here to let thoughts come into your mind. Is there anything that you're excited about? Worried about? Happy about? Unsure about? Let a thought float around in your head like a cloud, just letting it be there. Now you can decide what to do with that thought. Is it something that is important to you, or do you want to let it go?

- Now try this with another thought. Let it float into your head, and decide what you would like to do with it. You have the power to choose what happens to your thoughts. They are just like clouds that you can let float by or you can give a name to. Sometimes, a thought might come up that you don't like, and you can also choose to change that while it is floating in your mind. For example, you might have a thought that makes you worried. You can change the way you see this thought so that you can feel good about it, or you can also just let it go.

25. HOUSEWORK

Not many people enjoy doing chores. They can feel like thankless repetitive tasks that simply get on your nerves. But if you do the task mindfully, really thinking about it as you go, even if it brings up negativity, you will find it a more fulfilling experience. No matter what you're doing, if you are more present throughout, you will get more from the moment, effectively making it much more enjoyable.

As Thich Nhat Hanh said (*tinybuddha.com/blog*): *"To my mind, the idea that doing dishes is unpleasant can occur only when you aren't doing them…I enjoy taking my time with each dish, being fully aware of the dish, the water, and each movement of my hands. I know that if I hurry in order to eat dessert sooner, the time of washing dishes will be unpleasant and not worth living. That would be a pity, for each minute, each second of life is a miracle."*

Here are **some tips to make chores a more mindful experience**:

While washing dishes, tune in to:

- Your breath as you wash the dishes
- The temperature of the water on your hands
- The sensations and smell of the soap and bubbles
- The repetitive movements and motions involved with washing the dishes
- The wonder of having clean dishes ready to use at your next meal

While sweeping the floor, notice:

- How it makes your body feel, how your muscles stretch
- The sound of the broom's bristles
- The look of where you're brushing
- And repeat the mantra: *"I sweep the floor with attentiveness, and I sweep my mind."*

While doing the laundry:

- Notice the texture of the fabrics.
- Notice the patterns on each item of clothing.
- Notice the way the towels feel when they are fresh out of the dryer.
- Notice the colors of the clothing, and perhaps create new matches as you see how the articles may be able to work together.

- As you hang clothes to dry, notice how wet they are and get curious about how the color or weight will change once they are dry.

- If it's fresh out of the dryer, pay extra attention to the heat coming from the clothes and the fresh smell.

- Notice each and every detail as you fold shirt after shirt and sock after sock.

- Take a cleansing breath after you finish folding each article of clothing, offering gratitude that you have clean clothes to fold and wear, and sheets to sleep on.

26. NATURE

Nature is a wonderful place to be mindful. There's something about the sights, the sounds, and the smells that can really calm you down. Going out and experiencing nature might not be something that you already do, you may need to incorporate five minutes every single day for this exercise. Give it a try for a week and see how much better and more connected to the earth you feel.

Here are some tips on **getting the most out of your walk or moment standing in nature**, to combine with your mindful breathing:

- Allow yourself to spend time with your environment and nature.

- Be intentional when you connect and become present with your environment and nature around you. This will make it easier to be intentional as you observe your internal reactions and sensations as you connect to your environment and nature.

- Bring your awareness to the sounds, smells, sensations, and sights of your environment. It's normal for your mind to wander. Just shift your attention back to your immediate environment or mindful breathing.

- Enrich your experience with fresh insight by using mindfulness to connect with nature.

27. DRIVING

Driving is a regular activity that we take part in, that we don't do mindfully. It's very hard, especially when traveling on the same route a lot, not to go into autopilot and start thinking about other things. Once you get into the habit of driving without mindfulness, it's very easy to continually slip into that. Not only is this unhelpful, it's also very dangerous. Without giving your car and the driving experience the respect and attention it deserves and needs, accidents happen.

Of course, it is not advised that you close your eyes to focus on your breath, but **there are some things you can do**:

- Direct your focus, first, by driving in silence. Try to direct yourself beyond how strange this might feel, but your attention will sharpen. Your reflexes will work faster, which can make your driving safer overall.

- With your sharpened attention, take note of the sensations within your body; your muscles, your level of comfort. This attention and awareness will give you the space to change what is uncomfortable.

- Intentionally drive slower than the posted speed limit. You may not realize it, but that constant urge to drive faster and faster stresses your body even more.

- Pay attention to your emotions and feelings. Do you notice the inherently competitive nature that driving generates? Allow the ways that other people drive to pass you by without judgement. Maintain awareness of yourself and your driving. Be careful, pay attention – intentionally using the mirrors, even if you don't agree with how others drive. Recognize that you only have control over yourself.

- At each stop, take an opportunity to perform a mindful check-in with your body. Try to focus on the world just outside your car as you're stopped.

- Take the few moments before you start the engine and after you stop the engine to sit in stillness and silence. Take a couple mindful breaths, inhaling peace and exhaling tension.

28. USE YOUR PHONE

You might think that your phone is the enemy to mindfulness, that it will distract you and constantly drag you from the present moment, but if you use it right, it can actually assist you. Rather than allowing your phone to consume your life, you need to control usage of it so you only use it when you need to.

Here are **some great tips to help you with this**:

- Turn off the notifications. This might seem like a scary concept at first, but it can help you to pick up your phone less, and only when you want to look at it. Do you really need to see everything that happens on social media right away?

- Use silent. Get some peace by turning your phone to silent for specific times during the day. Especially when you're being mindful.

- Don't have your phone out all the time. This will help you to resist the urge to touch it constantly.

- Have a lock screen that reminds you about mindfulness. Write across the screen 'why am I in your hand?' so you really have to think about this.

- Set timers so your phone will alert you when you have been on a certain app for too long – most new phones have this feature.

- Turn the screen to grayscale so it's less interesting.

- Don't have all your apps on the open screen so they are harder to access, making it less appealing.
- Turn your phone off an hour before you go to bed.

29. MUSIC

Music can sometimes be a distraction from mindfulness and living in the present moment, because it's very easy to lose ourselves in our imagination with the sounds; it's very easy to drift off into a past moment or to think of something that you want to happen. But if you use music in the right way, it can actually assist in anchoring you.

Many online meditation sites actually use music as a part of their practice, because if you really focus and zone in on each sound, then it can actually be an amazing way to center yourself in the present moment.

Here is **some advice to help you with this**:

- Select a style of music that you enjoy listening to, that you can focus on without distraction. Sit in a comfortable position – any position where you are most likely to relax.

- Start mindful breathing. Use five breaths to get grounded. Focus on the sensations moving within your body. Visualize breathing in peace and breathing out tension.

- Maintain focus on your music, just the sounds in the present. It is normal for music to bring up memories and various feelings. Allow yourself to observe these thoughts, but don't judge them. If you feel yourself getting carried away, bring your awareness back to your breathing.

- Notice what has changed in the emotional, mental, and physical sensations of your body because you allowed yourself to sit with the music. Awareness and relaxation will allow your mind to be quieter, more at peace, even after the music is done. Enjoy the silence that follows the song, take a couple deep breaths, then go back to the day's activities with the intention of taking this new awareness and relaxation with you throughout the day.

30. CANDLE MEDITATION

Candle flames are hypnotic; they have a captivating way of dancing and darting, full of colors and excitement. Because of this, it can be a great way to anchor yourself and experience five minutes of mindfulness. The light has a way of drawing out positivity and helping you to feel calm. You might feel silly staring at a candle flame, but it's a wonderful way to prevent yourself from getting distracted from the outside world.

Here is **a great exercise to help you with this**:

- Sit comfortably, light your candle, and begin to breathe mindfully, focusing only on the way the breath feels traveling in and out of your body.

- Focus on the flame. Breathe in deeply through your nose. Let your stress and tension evaporate as you slowly exhale. Continue mindful breathing, breathing in peace and breathing out the day's stress and worry.

- Keep a comfortable posture, with a straight back, and use your breath – feeling your stomach expand as you inhale and contract as you exhale – to maintain that posture.

- As your mindful breathing takes on a steady pace, bring your focus back to the burning candle. Soften your gaze, note the flame's variety of colors. Concentrate on how the flame moves. Simply observe the candle and its flame without passing judgement, just observe.

- Allow any active thoughts, simply acknowledge them, then imagine them floating away on the flame's smoke.
- After five minutes, shift your focus away from the flame and expand this awareness to the entire room.
- Take five slow, mindful breaths, then go on with your day – calmer and more aware.

31. STOP AND SHOWER

Showering is something that we do all the time, pretty much every day, and it's a time that we can use to be mindful rather than thinking about everything that we need to do over the day or stressing about something that has already happened.

There is a lot going on in the shower that we can use to center ourselves. The feel of the water on our skin, the sounds it makes, the smell of the shampoo or shower gel, or the sight of the water as it falls.

Here is **a great exercise for this** that can be done in either the bath or shower:

- Sight. What can you see? Watch the water run over your skin if you're in the shower – or if you're in the bath, look at the patterns on the surface of the water. Make ripples and watch them grow.

- Smell. Close your eyes and think about each of the different scents you can smell – lavender, chamomile, lemon, soap. Choose your favorite fragrance and focus on it.

- Touch. Think about how the water feels against your skin. Take a moment to think about your body too – are there any tense muscles? Let them relax and allow the tension to drift away.

- Sound. What can you hear? Pick out the individual sounds one by one – water running, bird sounds, people talking, traffic.

- Allow yourself to remain for a while, just enjoying the moment before you get out of the shower/bath and have a great day.

32. DRINK WATER

Most of us need to include more water in our diets because it's very beneficial to our health. It helps our brains function better. It's great with assisting weight control. It can also prevent headaches, stomachaches, and cramps.

This is something that doesn't take a long time, yet, somehow, we don't find enough time to do it. If it's something that we decide to add into our schedule, then why not combine it with mindfulness? By mindfully drinking the water, it will encourage you to keep up the habit.

Here are **some tips to help you consume water more mindfully**:

- Start by really looking at your glass, experience the cool sensation through the smooth glass, then slow down your breathing and start breathing mindfully. Focus on your glass, the water inside, and let any thoughts that drop in pass you by. Notice the water's clarity as you inhale. Send away your tension or stress as you exhale. Allow your mind to feel this clarity and peace.

- Sip it slowly, feel the water cool you as it travels through your body. Pause to breathe after each sip. Make the intention to carry this mindfulness with you throughout the day.

- After you finish, slowly set down the empty glass and keep breathing mindfully as you clean it to prepare for using it again.

33. LAUGHTER

There is something magically uplifting about laughter. The sound has such positive connotations about it that it makes you feel much better without trying too hard. The idea of doing a laughter meditation might fill you with dread, and it isn't for everyone. It might be worth just giving it a go, because as soon as you lose the self-consciousness that comes with it, you will receive endless mental and physical benefits.

The laughter meditation is an emotional release that brings you into the present moment and makes you much more aware of everything going on around you, melting away the stress at the same time.

"The science of laughter – though still preliminary – suggests that it has tremendous benefits for our health and psychological well-being," Emma Seppälä writes in Scope, Stanford Medicine's blog (*scopeblog.stanford.edu/2015/04/09/seven-ways-laughter-can-improve-your-well-being*).

Here is **a great mindful laughter meditation** for you:

- 1 minute: Stand with your feet hip-width apart and stretch your arms high above your head. Rock your body side-to-side from your torso, then bend over and touch your hands to your feet. Next, massage your jaw and yawn at least two times to loosen your mouth and relax the muscles in your jaw.

- 2 minutes: Find a comfortable position to sit or stand. Start by slightly smiling and then begin laughing without too much effort. Move to deep belly laughs. (Hint: try different types of laughs to encourage your true laugh to come through. Even if it begins as a forced feeling, most people find the forced laughter catalyzes authentic laughter in no time.)

- 2 minutes: Sit or lie on the floor in stillness and silence. Be mindful of what comes up for you – how your body feels, emotions that present themselves, and thoughts that arise. (*Optional*: share what comes up with a trusted friend or write it down in a journal.)

34. TAME CRAVINGS

Mindfulness can also help you to tackle certain issues, such as cravings. Wanting is a typical state of mind and very common with our busy lifestyles. Wanting a fast fix to issues such as hunger to fit in our hectic days seems easier in terms of a short-term solution, where a long-term solution is a separate issue. Cravings and fixing those cravings with what you want isn't giving your body what it needs.

Mindfulness can help with this. By calming the mind and existing with inner peace, you become more in tune with what your body needs. You're less likely to grab that quick fix because your mindset is completely different.

Here is **an effective exercise that can help you directly with overcoming this particular issue**, so if it's something you struggle with, then give it a try; see what positive effect you can get from it:

- Sit in a comfortable position and tune in to your body's sensations with a mindful check-in. Notice how your body feels in this moment. Is there any tension? Then, focus on your breathing.

- After you've brought your focus to the present, label the cravings that come into your mind. Allow any urges to come to mind. Something pleasant or unpleasant, whatever you feel like you need to deal with, or something you haven't done or had in a long time. Mindfully check-in and explore what this urge really feels like moving through your body.

- Explore how the feeling moves through your body by trying to identify where it exists within your body. Focus on the sensations, maybe even try to name them. Can you determine a specific location where the urge appears in your body?

- Now just take a moment to focus on this awareness of your body. How does it feel to become aware of these bodily sensations? This awareness is the first step to no longer being a slave to your urges or cravings. When you can explore them with mindfulness, you begin to free up every moment.

- Finally, just sit with this awareness. Make the intention to carry this awareness with you, so you can be on the lookout. This way, you can take control of those cravings and urges, positive or negative. Remember to stay open-minded to diving in and exploring each sensation that will appear with these cravings and urges.

35. AROMATHERAPY

Aromatherapy is great to use with mindfulness; the two things complement each other well. The scents aromatherapy uses are pleasant and uplifting, often calming too. While there are mindful exercises that focus on the senses, there aren't many that focus solely on the nose and smell, which makes this exercise exciting.

Here are **some tips for you**:

- Introduce a pleasant aroma into your environment by placing a few essential oil drops in a water diffuser, brewing fresh coffee, or cutting a lemon in half.

- Close your eyes if you like and breathe normally. Settle into a comfortable position. Notice how you are feeling in this moment.

- Pay attention to the aroma and any other sensations that are happening for you right now. Name the scent and any sensations that are happening for you. Is your body tense or relaxed? Are there any particular spots of tension, like your shoulders or lower back?

- Think about a color or shape that you would associate with the aroma that is now filling your environment.

- Focus on your breathing. What memories or recollections can you associate with this particular aroma?

- How would you describe how you are feeling in this moment?

36. HUG

Hugging is a wonderful activity with many health benefits to it. Having this wonderful, uplifting, reassuring contact with another person can calm you down, release your endorphins – which are the chemicals of happiness, relax your muscles, reduce stress, and boost your immune system, to name just a few benefits.

When you combine mindfulness with hugging, it can connect you with the earth and other people, bringing an intense sense of inner peace that can make your day so much better. It really helps to build your bond with the other person and connects you to yourself as well. What better way to experience a mindful moment with another person?

Here is a great **hugging mindfulness exercise** for you:

- Choose who you wish to hug. A family member, a lover, a friend, a child, a teddy, or even a tree.

- Recognize the presence of one another. Smile at each other while taking in three deep, mindful breaths to anchor yourselves.

- Step into the embrace and hug. Take three mindful breaths as you hold the embrace.

- Take your first breath, and use that time to become aware of the present and how you feel.

- Take your second breath, and use that time to become aware of the other person's presence and how you feel about that.

- Take your third breath, and use that time to become aware that the both of you are here, right now in this moment. Focus on having gratitude and happiness for this mindful moment together.
- Then, release the embrace and smile at each other to share that gratitude and happiness.

37. HOT CHOCOLATE

There is nothing more comforting than a mug of hot chocolate. There's something about the warmth and smell that instantly fills you with happiness. If you love a hot, comforting drink, then **it's something that you can include in your mindfulness**, as shown by this exercise:

- Quietly and slowly breathe in through your nose as you smell (or imagine smelling) a mug of hot chocolate.

- Exhale by blowing through your mouth to cool the beverage off.

- Repeat this four times.

38. CAMERA EYES

The camera eyes exercise takes mindful observation to a whole new level, allowing you to more **deeply engage with your vision of your surroundings**. By actively engaging in what you're seeing around you, you will immediately be drawn into the present moment and you won't allow distractions to grab you:

- Take a few mindful breaths and relax, either sitting or standing.

- Look around you for a minute or so and notice everything you can.

- Close your eyes and visualize all you can remember of what you saw around you.

- Open your eyes again and compare what you see to what you remembered.

39. SOUNDS

Using your ears and concentrating on sounds is another way to use your senses to help to ground you. By focusing on this one sense, you can properly engage with it and take a moment to just **be in the moment with the noises around you**:

- Get in a comfortable position and take five deep breaths. Once you feel grounded, close your eyes.

- Pick one sound and focus on it. Notice everything you can about this sound and its qualities. Is it soft or loud? High-pitched or low-pitched? Intermittent or constant? Is it tinny or full-sounding? How does it vary as you listen to it?

- Do this again with another sound – repeat as many times as you like.

- If distracting thoughts pop up, gently bring your attention back to this sound. Keep listening for about a minute.

- Now focus on your breathing again and simply allow the sounds to fall on your ears. Don't focus on any one in particular or get caught up in any.

- Once you are ready, open your eyes and return to the room.

40. FEEL THE AIR

The air is a great sensation, if you really feel it. It's refreshing and uplifting, it connects you to nature in a lovely way, and it brings you into the present moment – if you allow it to. Taking a moment to do **this exercise can really help you just enjoy five minutes of mindfulness**, feeling and experiencing the sensation of the breeze around you:

- Stand or sit still and notice the air around you.

- Try and notice the temperature of the air and what it feels like against your skin. Notice the movement of the air. Notice what you feel. Can you feel the movement of the air on your skin? You may feel the sensation of the air on the fine hairs on your body.

- Allow yourself to just pay attention to the sensation of the air and how it feels. As you focus completely on the air surrounding you, you may notice minute changes in the air.

- Allow yourself to be open to the experience of the air around you.

41. WAITING IN LINE

Waiting in line can be a very unpleasant experience, especially if we are busy and have a million other places that we would rather be. But, you're in that line for a reason. There is something that you need to do or get, and you can't escape it, so why not use the time wisely and create a moment for mindfulness.

Here is **a tip using the word WAIT to assist you**:

- **Watch**: What's going on around you? What can you see and hear? Can you smell anything? Mindfully observe your surroundings.

- **Accept**: You might not like waiting in line, but there's something very powerful about just accepting the moment for what it is. You can't change it, you're here for a reason, so just take the time for what it is. It doesn't matter how many things you have left on your 'to do' list. You can't do them right now, so worry about them when you can.

- **Investigate**: Observe your thoughts. What is going on inside your mind? Are you telling yourself stories and turning this into a much bigger deal than it is? Noticing that gives these thoughts much less power over you.

- **Tend**: Tend to yourself with compassion. Tell yourself, *"Yes, this is hard right now. What can I do to be kind to myself?"* Use the moment wisely, maybe talk to another person in the line or simply have some mindful appreciation.

42. FEEL THE MATERIAL

Touch meditation is another way to anchor yourself. If you often find your mind wandering, then **having something to feel can assist you**. Material is good for this because there will always be something around you or on you. If you can find an unusual material to work with, then even better:

- Sit on the floor with your feet planted, rest one hand against your chest and the other on your tummy, then close your eyes.

- Take a long breath in; count to four. Release that deep breath as you count to four. Repeat.

- Now, pick a material. Whether it's the feel of the chair or something that you're wearing. Focus on the texture and the way that it feels. Does it evoke any thoughts or emotions? Simply observe these sensations.

- Does the material have an aroma? What does it smell like?

- Take a few moments to simply observe, then open your eyes and take a look at the material. Think about the colors and any patterns.

- As soon as you feel like it, allow your awareness to extend to the rest of your body, then the rest of the room.

43. DRAWING

Drawing and coloring have become very popular mindful activities recently, with lots of people enjoying these calming, creative tasks. But to really do it mindfully, you have to ensure that you're fully engaged in the drawing or coloring for at least five minutes. Focus on the feel on the pencil in your hand, notice the sound it makes against the paper, pay attention to the colors.

Here is **an exercise for you** to try:

- Consider the colored pencil in front of you and pick it up and hold it. Take your time and give attention to its weight and the balance as it sits in your hand.

- What does it feel like to be curious about this object?

- How did you grip your pencil? What does it feel like in your hand?

- Take a deep breath at your own pace. Did you notice a smell?

- Breathe again, this time, turning your attention to the air filling your lungs and take notice of any scents.

- Without judgement, turn your attention to the color of your pencil – notice the vibrant color encased by wood. You might be disappointed in the color of your pencil, but just like all the feelings in your body have a role, all the colors have an important place in the color spectrum. Now let your fingers explore the smooth texture of your pencil and the rough exposed wood near the point.

- Turn your attention inward and notice what you are feeling.

- Do you notice impatience? Do you feel a sense of anticipation to color? What do your hands feel like as they wait to color? What emotions are coming up? You don't have to change them, just notice.

- Now, hold your pencil in one hand and direct your attention to your paper. What do you notice in your body as you face a blank page with defined lines? When you color, will you choose to befriend those boundaries or will you choose to treat the paper as though there are no boundaries?

- You have a choice. Notice which option you are inclined towards and allow yourself to wonder what it would be like to choose the other.

- Take another deep breath at your own pace and give yourself a moment to anticipate coloring. What will it feel like to transfer this living color in your hand to the page in front of you?

- Know that you will NOT finish coloring this page today and that is okay. Bless this quiet moment you are taking to enjoy coloring, with all your senses, in this small part of your day.

- Now that you are familiar with your pencil and the space before you, choose a spot on your paper and gently place your pencil against it, just barely making contact with the paper. Now begin to color the page.

- Keep coloring, noticing the sound of your pencil on the page, the texture of your paper, and any other sensations rising to your attention. Alternate coloring with pressure and gently tracing your pencil across the page. What changes about the color when you change pressure? What changes in your grip or in your breathing? Just notice.

- Take the next few minutes to color, paying attention to your body, all it senses in this space, and the miracle of the transfer of color as it moves from your pencil to the page.

44. READING

Reading is a wonderfully calming exercise, but it can also be something that we do on autopilot, without really engaging in the activity. **Try this way of reading** to see if it makes it more enjoyable for you:

- Read a short piece, maybe one page, quietly and then consider the phrase that stands out the most for you. Repeat that phrase to yourself. More than once, if you like. Think about how it makes you feel. What ideas, feelings, images, or memories come to mind?

- Take another look at the words in that phrase. Is there a word or more that have a meaning beyond its typical use? Think about the meaning that word or words give to the entire passage of what you're reading.

- Keep the phrase in the front of your mind and read the entire passage again. Does is it sound or feel different? Notice how your relationship to the passage has changed.

45. GIVE MINDFUL ATTENTION TO KIDS

Kids often struggle to get attention in this world, where we are all obsessed with our technology. When they talk to us, we are distracted by our phones. As soon as they are playing, we are busy looking at our emails or cleaning the house. When it's bedtime or bath time, that's a stress because we have so much else to do – it's no wonder they turn to technology as well.

This isn't something to punish yourself over, because it's a trap we're all lost in. Instead of worrying about it, pledge to give you and your child or children at least five minutes of your undivided attention where you can mindfully listen to them. This can help improve their self-worth, their behavior, and their own attention.

Here is a quick exercise to try **to help improve your focus and attention**:

- Focus on an object placed in front of you.
- Concentrate on the object for as long as possible.
- Notice when your mind wanders, acknowledge those thoughts, then bring it back to the object.
- Use mindfulness to extend how long you can focus on the object. This will boost your ability to focus.

46. BATH

Mindful bathing is becoming a very popular way to really enjoy bath time and to get the absolute most out of it. By really paying attention to what you're doing, instead of daydreaming or looking at your phone, you can make it a calming, relaxing experience that brings with it a great sense of inner peace. This can be a wonderful way to start or end your day.

Here is **an exercise to help with this**:

- Start with some mindful breathing as you anchor yourself to the present moment, then start in silence.

- Bring all your attention into the bathroom. Notice the colors, any sounds you can hear inside and outside the room, the feel of the water on your skin, the way that you feel.

- Establish a new pattern of washing your body and be attentive to each detail. Draw your mind to each body part as you wash it.

- Without luxuriating in the feel of the water, be mindful of its pure quality and direct your mind into an attitude of gratitude.

- Once you have finished washing every part of you with care and kindness, return to breathing mindfully, before allowing the rest of the world back in.

47. SKIN CARE

Almost everyone has a skin care routine. This could be a long and complex process involving all sorts of lotions or creams, or simply a wash, but if it's something that you do every single day, then bringing some mindfulness to it will make the experience a much more positive one, rather than something rushed while you worry about everything else.

Here is **a new routine for you to try**. Adjust it to suit how you take care of your own skin:

- CLEANSE – run the water to a pleasing temperature and, with closed eyes, splash some on your face. Rub the cleansing lotion between your fingers, inhaling the smell, before applying it to your skin. Notice how slick the cleanser feels, and any sensations it brings to your skin. Be aware of all the residue being cleaned away. Tell yourself: *"I can be or do or have anything."*

- MIST – apply toner slowly and focus on the sensation of your skin hydrating. Pause to breathe in the new scent and experience universal love.

- MOISTURIZING MASSAGE – Before your skin dries, rub the massaging serum between your fingers and, with your eyes closed, rub it into your skin. Massage while noticing the texture of your face. Appreciate the loving touch.

- NOURISH, REFINE, & PROTECT – Apply face cream with a nice smell, while telling yourself: *"I allow myself to resonate with these essences."* Take deep breaths and focus on what you feel.

- AFFIRM – See the glow of your skin. Make eye contact with your reflection, and say: *"I am brilliant, radiant, and beautiful."*

48. YOGA

If you enjoyed the mindful stretches that we talked about earlier, then why not extend it and include some yoga in your exercise and mindfulness routine? Or, perhaps, yoga is something that you're already doing and you want to be more mindful with it. Either way, why not try really noticing how your body feels during these stretches? Don't judge yourself if you can't always do the poses exactly right; be content with what you can do today.

You may want to join a class or learn about the yoga poses on your own. Whatever you decide, here are **some great tips to get you started**:

- Schedule some uninterrupted time for yourself, where you can be focused on the present the entire time.

- Start with a mindful check-in to see how you and your body are feeling.

- Keep in mind that muscles require time. Build your endurance and strength by increasing your workout slightly every week.

- Allow yourself to take steps backward. There will be times when you cannot progress at your desired rate. This is normal.

- Setbacks will happen. This is also normal. Give yourself an opportunity to really get in tune with yourself and grow in your new bodily awareness.

- Finish with another mindful check-in to see how your mind and body responded to the yoga workout. Take a moment to note what worked, what didn't, and what you can work on during the next workout.

If this is something that you want to get started with, Palouse Mindfulness (*palousemindfulness.com/meditations/yoga1.html*) has a lot of resources for trying mindful yoga and mindful movements.

49. APPS

Since your phone is one of those things that's with you all the time, why not download some apps to get into the mind-set of mindfulness. You don't have to use just one, and you can change as often as you want, using trial and error to assist you. You might find it easier to hear someone giving you the guidelines for your meditation rather than trying to keep your mind on the right track yourself.

Here are **some of the more popular mindfulness apps** for you to try:

Calm

Headspace

Stop, Breathe, and Think

10% Happier

Insight Timer

50. JUST BE

Mindfulness is a moment to just be. To be in the moment and to just exist. Finding somewhere that makes you happy and calm is the most effective way to do this, because it will leave you with a strong sense of peace and joy before you even begin. Positivity at the beginning of the meditation will breed even more positivity at the end.

Find somewhere new, or somewhere familiar, that fills you with happiness, and have a go at this exercise:

- Sit in a comfortable position, with your back straight.
- Place your feet flat on the floor, shoulder width apart.
- Rest your right hand, palm up, in your lap against your abdomen.
- Rest your left hand on top of your right hand, so the back of the left hand rests on the palm of the right hand.
- Touch the tips of your thumbs together.
- Drop your chin toward your chest slightly.
- Bring the tip of the tongue up to rest lightly behind your upper teeth, against the roof of your mouth.
- Look straight ahead of you, keeping your eyes open and relaxed without staring at any particular object or spot.
- Breathe in slowly through your nose so that your stomach muscles extend, as if it is being filled up with your breath.
- Pause for a count of three when your stomach feels almost fully extended.
- Now, press your stomach in, as if it will touch your spine, to let your breath back out through your nose.
- Continue the breathing process, inhale slowly, pause for count of three, then exhale slowly for count of four. Try practicing this through five cycles of mindful breathing.

Morning Mindfulness Rituals

51. WAKING UP

Waking up isn't always easy, especially if you have to get up for something you aren't looking forward to, such as a stressful day at work. Taking some time for you when you first wake up is a good way to start your day. Waking up and having your brain racing at the speed of light will have you on edge and irritated before you even begin. That isn't healthy and won't create a good path for the rest of your day. Starting positive will at least give you the chance of having a better day.

Here is **a good mindfulness practice to start your day right**, which needs to be done as soon as you wake up:

- Create a relaxing space to practice five minutes of mindfulness. Use quiet music, some diffused essential oils, or burning incense to set the mood.

- Dress in comfortable clothes, or you could simply stay in your pajamas, which could make this waking-up exercise a more functional transition from sleep to being awake.

- Take a comfortable position with your back straight.

- Use a timer, set for five minutes, to make sure you don't run late for work or any appointments.

- Begin by taking five deep breaths. Visualize breathing in peace and breathing out tension.

- Chose an object from around you to concentrate on. Examine the object's textures and colors, the sounds of the music you selected, or the aroma of the oils or incense; you could even focus on a favorite affirmation that will put you in a positive mind-set.

- Maintain focus on the selected object, while sustaining your mindful breathing, where each breath in is filling you with peace and each exhale dissipates stress.

- You can keep this transition between sleeping and waking up positive by gently bringing yourself back to your breathing and focus when you have thoughts or feelings, even sensations in your body or distracting sounds from your environment. All of these are natural while you try to practice mindfulness, just remember you can take control of what you focus on.

- After the timer rings, make the intention to carry this new awareness with you throughout the day.

52. SMILE IN THE MIRROR

In our busy lives, we don't actually spend much time looking in the mirror. Or if we do, it's when we're tired in the morning, barely paying any attention, just getting ready on autopilot while the day rushes past. When we do see ourselves, it's usually just to check one area or to criticize ourselves.

Why not change this up a bit? Turn it into five minutes of self-love instead? Smile at yourself and remind yourself that you are a good person, with positivity and something to offer the world. There is something very uplifting about a smile, so give it a try.

Here is **a great exercise** for this:

- Sit comfortably in front of the mirror. Now, take a look at yourself while breathing mindfully.

- What do you notice? Look at yourself with kindness and without judgement.

- Start by putting a small smile on your face. Then, slowly make it wider. With each breath, make the smile extend ear to ear.

- Hold a comfortable smile as you breathe deep through your nose, in and out. Repeat this twice.

- Keep doing this for five minutes. Notice how it makes your face look and how it makes you feel. What body sensations does it bring up? What emotions and thoughts?

Mindfulness Habits Before Sleep

53. SLEEP BETTER

There are so many reasons why we need a good night's sleep; it isn't just to stop us from feeling tired. Insomnia can affect our mental and physical well-being in a number of different ways including stress, weight, memory, mood, blood pressure, our hearts, and pain, just to name a few.

If sleep is a real issue for you, then there are some things that you can do to help yourself. A nighttime routine is a good place to begin, where you can ensure you're doing the same things before you get into bed, preparing your body for sleep. No screens for an hour before bed can also help get rid of restlessness. The light of the screens keeps our brains active and prevents deep sleep. Caffeine is also the enemy of sleep, so avoid it late in the day.

Mindfulness can also help. Switching your thoughts off and being in the present moment last thing at night before going to bed is really useful. Here is **a way to help you with this**:

- Lie down in a comfortable position with your hands resting softly on your belly.

- Notice the sensation of your breath going in and out of your body as your belly rises and falls. If any thoughts or emotions creep in to distract you, as soon as you notice this, just gently bring your attention back to your breathing.

- Focus on the physical sensations in your feet. They don't need to be moved or wiggled, just think about how they feel right now. The feel of the bed covers, the pressure in the mattress, etc.

- Move up to the lower leg, the knees, the thighs. If there is any tension, try to relax the muscles.

- Notice the buttocks, pelvis, belly, abdomen. Are there any sensations here? There may even be tightness related to emotions. Try to relax this as much as you can.

- The same for your back and shoulders. Stress is often carried here, so if there is any tightness, try to loosen the muscles.

- Move up through the neck and face, to the top of your head. Once you have observed everything, it's time to bring your awareness to your body as a whole. Does it feel better now without all of the tension?

- For the rest of the five minutes, focus on your breath. With your body more relaxed, your mind may wander less, but even if it does, gently bring your attention back to your breath. If it's a useful anchor for your attention, you can count breaths, breathing in, one, breathing out, one, breathing in, two, breathing out, two. When you reach ten, start at one again.

- If counting becomes a distraction, then just stay with the sensation of breathing – wherever you feel the breath entering or leaving your body, or the rising or falling of your belly and chest. Continue on your own now, counting breaths up to ten, patiently returning your attention whenever you become distracted. If you lose track of counting, that's fine. Start over wherever you last remember.

54. SHUT DOWN

Shutting down can be really hard, especially at the end of the day when you're trying to go to sleep. There's something about the end of the day and lying down in bed seems to bring up all kinds of negative emotions and thoughts. The later into the night it gets, the harder it can be to close this off, which is why **shutting down mindfulness exercises can be really helpful.**

You can try this:

- Complete any complex tasks long before bedtime, then use relaxation methods to get your mind prepared for sleep.
- Help your body prepare for sleep by dimming the lights at the same time each night.
- This includes anything with a screen, because their blue light will keep your brain awake.
- Start a mindfulness method, where you are sitting comfortably and taking note of your breathing, ten minutes before bedtime.
- Do a mindful check-in and take note of any tension or pressure. Relax any tense muscles and acknowledge any negative emotions without judgement. Simply let them pass you by as you tune in to your body and its sensations.
- Climb into bed, then start mindful breathing. Close your eyes and keep using mindful breathing. Let any thoughts that appear be and pass by you without focusing on them.

Productivity Mindfulness Habits

55. WRITE YOUR JOURNEY

Writing about anything can be done mindfully. If this is something that you want to try, but you don't know where to start, **writing about your mindfulness journey can be really useful**. Not only is this a task that you can complete with mindfulness, it will also give you a record to look back on when you aren't sure whether you want to continue it or not. It can show your improvements, how it makes you feel, and how useful you think it is:

- When writing, stay in the present moment. Turn off your phone so you don't get distracted, create a moment of silence, and if your thoughts wander, simply notice them and bring them back to the task at hand.

- Start with mindful breathing to ground yourself.

- Notice the feel of your body in your seat, the sensation of the pen in your hand, how it feels when you begin to write.

- Don't get caught up in perfection, simply write from the heart; let your mind flow.

- Make mindful observations as you write.

- Keep this up, do it consistently.

56. SET DAILY INTENTIONS

There is something incredibly powerful about setting intentions for your day. This isn't a 'to do' list, something to stress you out; it's about you and how you would like to live this day. The intention can even be that you would like to go through the day more mindfully or with a more positive attitude.

This is something that's good to do in the morning, to start your day right, but you can also do a mindful check-in throughout the day to make sure that you're on the right path.

Here is **a great exercise for this**:

- What matters most to you today? (We can so easily get caught up in the momentum of the headlong rush of daily life – find ourselves putting one foot in front of the other. But, hey, you'll only live this day once, so what matters most?)

- What would you like to let go of? Are you holding resentments, regrets, grudges that no longer serve you?

- Who do you choose to be today? What are the values you choose to express and live today in the world?

- Carry this with you throughout the day.

57. DECLUTTER

Clutter is an enemy to mindfulness for a lot of people. It's a constant stress, a reminder of things you need to do, and it can also make you cling to painful memories without even realizing it. If your space isn't calming you and making you feel happy, then you need to do something about it. It's better for your entire home to be a safe haven, to make you feel relaxed and full of joy, but if that isn't possible, then you need at least a room or an area that's just for you.

This might seem like a daunting task, and one you don't really want to face, but the long-term benefits of it will be endless. **Here are some tips** to help you:

- Even if the task feels overwhelming, don't start it with dread. Begin with some mindful breaths and take it as a clearing exercise. A cleansing for your soul.

- Do it in manageable bites. Five minutes a day, staying in the present moment, feeling every item, looking at it with care, taking note of the emotions you experience inside.

- Don't do it alone. If it feels like too much, get someone to help you.

- Use three boxes to work with – keep, throw away, donate.

- You can repurpose things if you know that you will use them, but if they no longer bring you any joy and you haven't used them for three years, it's time to get rid of them.

58. TRANSITION BREATHING

Transition breathing is simply taking a breath in between activities, to give us some separation. When we rush through each task, racing from one thing to the next, it's easy to lose ourselves, forget things, and become overwhelmed. If you constantly find yourself stressed, feeling like there is a massive weight on your shoulders, then it's time to give this a try. Every time you are about to change task, just take a blank, calming moment.

Here is **an exercise for you to try**:

- Put the previous task down. You can pick it up again later (if you wish).

- Bring your attention back to your breath.

- Pay attention to your breath and apply, if you like, the conscious thought of breathing in for three counts, holding for four counts, and breathing out for five. Repeat a few times or for as long as you require until you are refocused and present with your breath and your body as the diaphragm and lungs do their jobs.

- Take the breaths purposely and bring your attention to the next task you need to attend to.

- Take a moment to be present with the intention of this task. (What is it you want to achieve, how will you do this, what will you be focusing on, how will you be present, how much time will you honor this task?)

- Be aware of your mind and your sensations in your whole body as these intention(s) are set. (Make sure they are right for you.)

- Now transition to the task. Be mindful, aware of your breathing, thoughts, behavior, and attention as you move forward.

- Repeat as you finish this task and move to the next.

59. BATCH YOUR TASKS

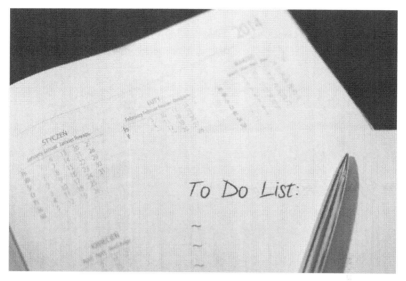

Flittering from one task to the next, constantly changing what you're doing to try and keep on top of things is actually a worse way to be productive. Many people who have tried batching their tasks – i.e., grouping a list of similar tasks together in a time block to keep your concentration – have been very successful.

By not swapping and changing all the time, you will be much less likely to forget things or miss it off your 'to do' list. You will also feel much calmer and more in control.

If your list of things to do keeps getting bigger and bigger and more out of control, then **it might be wise to give batching a go**. It will only take five minutes to get your list in order, and it will make a massive difference to your day:

- Put together your 'to do' list.

- Batch tasks by their location or function. Ask yourself how certain tasks are similar.

- Break your day down, by time of day or the hour, then assign a task category to each segment of time.

Of course, this might not work out exactly to plan, especially at first. Life might get in the way, or you may find that it takes longer to do something than you planned. Don't beat yourself up about this, just take a mindful breath and rearrange.

Here is some advice for **what categories you can use to organize your** new life:

- **Email**. You only need to check your email once per day. Or twice. Once in the morning, once in the afternoon. That might seem like an impossible task, but if you set an automatic reply to let people know that you will get back to them as soon as you can, then you will find this liberating because you aren't stuck to your phone or desk all the time.

- **Reading**. Set a time aside during the day or week to get all the reading done that you need to. Without distractions, this task will be much easier and more effective. Set different times for different reading materials, such as books, magazines, research, or work-related texts.

- **Blogging**. Schedule your posts to go out through the week, to save you having to worry about it each day.

- **Calls**. Make a list of the people who call, and clear return calls at the same time each day. Returning calls in this way will free up time, especially if you can choose times when you and other people are the least busy.

- **Leisure**. Keep your time for entertainment toward the end of the day. This will help keep procrastination in check and motivate you to complete your work.

- **Assignments**. Try to get any assignments done in one setting, or as few as you can manage. This will ensure that it's the best it can be.

- **Computer Work**. Set times for the computer and times to go wireless to give your eyes a rest.

- **Cleaning**. Take the stress out of this chore by doing all the cleaning at one time. If you can, try choosing the same day during the week.

- **Shopping/Errands**. Visit the stores in one go to save on money and time.

- **Cooking**. Take one day per week to do the prep work for rest of the week's meals.

- **Classes**. See if you arrange your schedule to take multiple classes in the same day.

- **Free Time**. Try to rearrange as much of your work schedule, being housework, paid work, running errands, even seeing friends and family, and create a free day for yourself to relax and reflect on your goals and progress.

- **Thinking**. Try to get in the habit of setting aside time, each day or each week, to secure uninterrupted time to think – simply reflect on your life, your goals, and nothing more.

- **Planning**. Without planning, nothing gets done. Try to get in the habit of setting aside uninterrupted time to plan for your next project, idea, or goal.

- **Sleep**. Are you a chronic napper? This can turn into procrastination and a bad habit. It's better to sleep just once a day.

- **Repairs**. Make a list of the repairs around the house that you've been meaning to do. Plan to perform all these repairs on the same day or across a series of two or three days, back to back.

- **Social Contact**. Social media can dominate much of the time that could be spent doing other things on this list. Make an effort to actually meet people in person, which works better for batching time and is ultimately more satisfying.

- **'To Do' List**. Instead of always adding to the list and making it a mess, take notes of what you need to do throughout the day, but set aside some time to batch all your tasks for the following day.

- **Research**. Research is much more effective when done in batch rather than in little bits here and there.

60. POMODORO

The Pomodoro Technique is developed by Frances Cocirillo (_francescocirillo.com/pages/pomodoro-technique_) as a way to manage your time and manage your workload, ensuring that you get enough breaks to continue being functional. This is a great way to get on top of your 'to do' list and also become more mindful. Instead of racing against the clock and constantly feeling stressed.

Pomodoro is Italian for tomato and that's because it generally refers to the tomato timer often used in kitchens.

- Choose the task that you'll do.

- Use a timer and set it for five minutes.

- Be mindful of the work you are doing. Using all five of your senses to focus on and observe what is happening.

- After the timer goes off, pause and take one mindful breath. You can keep working this exercise, simply by restarting the timer. Use the timer and this exercise for up to twenty-five minutes.

This shorter time helps to eliminate distractions and to concentrate much better. Studies have suggested that this is a great way to stay on top of things, to stay productive, and also to remain grounded.

61. SLOW WORK

When we work under the constant pressure of time and deadlines, it's hard to imagine that slowing down could actually make you feel more productive, but actually it can, as studies have shown (_www.fastcompany.com/3057853/five-ways-working-more-slowly-can-boost-your-productivity_). Working slower, more mindfully, and with a better focus can also ensure that you don't make mistakes, so your work will be even better.

This idea of slow living is applied to many things, including eating (_www.precisionnutrition.com/all-about-slow-eating_), and it's designed to help calm our lives down, prevent stress, and give us a sense of inner peace, which is why combining it with mindfulness is a perfect mix.

Slowing down is daunting for many people, especially when they have so much work to do, but by taking more time over things, and even using the batching method as described before, you will get more done, suffer less distractions and procrastination, and most importantly, it will help you to create a much better work-life balance.

Here is **some great advice to help you with this**:

- Create a short daily schedule in the morning and calculate twice as much time for each point on this 'to do' list than you would estimate. Yes, that might seem scary, but by batching tasks, it will become much more manageable for you.

- Take breaks and use these short breaks for a moment of mindfulness. Use this to grab a hot drink and take a moment to yourself, talk to some colleagues and listen to them mindfully, do some mindful breathing.

- Be sure to avoid any multitasking. You should check your inbox only twice a day – not every five minutes. Email can easily take over your life, if you allow it to. Nothing sent via email is life or death, and by checking it less, you will have more time to yourself.

- Actively add relaxation periods to your day. A time to just do nothing; think, nothing, just live in the moment and enjoy mindful observation or appreciation.

- Be patient – this isn't always the easiest to implement, so be kind to yourself if it all goes wrong. If you find yourself getting stressed again, then take five minutes of mindfulness to calm yourself down again.

62. DIGITAL BREAK

Taking a break from technology is very important and something that we neglect a lot of the time. Even when we aren't on the computer, we are looking at our phone screens or watching television. It's rare to get a complete break from it. It's something that everyone should try to incorporate into their daily lives, even if it's for only five minutes a day.

Here are **some tips to help you with this**:

- Go for a walk without your phone. Mindfully be in nature for five minutes.

- Turn your phone off every Sunday or every evening.

- Pick two hours a day to put your phone on silent.

- Take a moment to have a hot drink in peace. Don't look at your screen as you do.

- Set an alarm to remind you to walk away from everything. Have a digital-free area in your home or office to relax in.

Here is **a breathing exercise to make the most of this digital break**:

- Use a timer and set it for five minutes. This way you can focus on the meditation without worrying about meditating and missing something important.

- Close your eyes and focus on relaxing by taking a few mindful breaths. Release tension and stress each time you exhale. Visualize the stress leaving your body, the tension draining away through your feet, or escaping and melting away from between your lips.

- Focus on just being. This is an easier way to clear your mind than trying to 'think of nothing.' If thoughts, feelings, or urges appear, acknowledge them, then allow them to float away. Gently bring your attention back to the present.

- Keep working on your focus, directing your attention to your body and your breathing. Maintain this until the timer goes off, then go back to your day de-stressed, focused, and relaxed.

63. REVIEW

Reviewing our behavior and our lives is something that we don't do very often, because we see it as something that we don't have the time for. But if a mindful exercise can give you five minutes to reflect, then **why not see where you are and where you want to be?** If this reveals that you aren't on the right path at the moment, then you can make the appropriate changes to ensure this happens. There's no better key to happiness than knowing you're working towards your goals and doing so in a way that embodies all of your values and everything that's important:

- Sit yourself in a comfortable position and start mindful breathing for about one minute.

- Begin to think about who and what is important to you.

- Consider what your goals are.

- Know where you are right now.

- Are these the same? Are you on the right path?

- Any thoughts or emotions that crop up while considering these things, simply observe them and let them slip away.

- Return to mindful breathing; focus only on your breath until a sense of calm overcomes you.

64. PLAN

Planning might seem like a paradox when mindfulness is all about living in the moment, but it's very important to also know where you're going to go next. Being mindful of the present moment doesn't mean that you need to ignore the past and the future, just don't get caught up in it. Making a plan can cause the present to be much clearer in your mind, it can also make your next steps easier to take.

Here is **some advice for you**:

- Set goals but let go of your expectations. It doesn't matter how much you plan, things might not work out, so while it's lovely to have a goal, don't obsess over the outcome. Thinking and worrying won't mean that you have more control over what happens, it just makes you enjoy the journey less.

- Plan for the future, but don't waste your time worrying about the future. Worrying is as bad as procrastination. Planning has intention behind it, and a purpose. Worry doesn't.

- Balance planning with action. Don't forget that planning isn't the be-all and end-all. You also need to take action to ensure that your plan comes to life.

65. EMAILING

Emailing can also be a mindful activity, when done right. Emailing is something that should be done with a more active mind, because it prevents mistakes being made or something being taken wrong at the other end of the email. **Take more care over it, and use these tips:**

- Write the email message with intention and loving kindness.

- Take a deep, mindful breath.

- Focus on the person receiving the email. How do you want that person to read this message? Are your words clearly delivering the message you want to send? Think about the message from their perspective.

- Read the written email message again.

- Rewrite your message if it's needed.

- When you're ready, when you think your message is clear, then hit Send.

66. SET YOUR ALARM FOR MINDFULNESS

Forgetting can be an enemy to mindfulness. You can suddenly remember that you haven't performed your mindful five minutes for the day. When you remember this, it can cause stress and make it something to worry about rather than enjoy.

Alarms throughout the day can be a great trigger to remind us to observe and breathe for a moment. If you can't manage five minutes all in one go, do five one-minute moments.

Here is some advice for **how to make the most of these minutes**:

- Focus on the present. Notice your body and your breathing.
- Shift your awareness to your thoughts and feelings. Don't try to name them or judge them, just be aware of them and any reactions you have to those thoughts or feelings.
- Detach from those feelings and gently bring yourself back to the present moment by focusing on your breathing, coming back to your affirmation.
- Try to generate a positive feeling within yourself, for yourself or the moment, such as peacefulness, loving kindness, acceptance, or relaxation.

Or:

- Use mindful breathing.
- Practice gratitude.
- Become aware of your mind.
- Bring yourself back to the present.
- Focus on the message you are sending yourself.
- Breathe in loving kindness and compassion.
- Embrace, accept the present.
- Release your sense of attachment.
- Relax tension in your muscles.
- Put a smile on your face.
- Shift your focus to the sensations of your breathing and body.

67. SIMPLIFY YOUR ROUTINE

Mornings can be a particularly stressful time, and if you find yourself rushing around like a headless chicken, then simplifying your routine can really help you to live a calmer life with more inner peace. If you start your day well, then the rest of the day is bound to follow. You at least have a chance of it being positive if you aren't stressed from the moment you wake up.

Plum Village (*plumvillage.org/mindfulness-practice/waking-up/*) suggests that you wake up with this mantra every day to incite positivity: *"Waking up this morning I smile, knowing there are 24 brand new hours before me. I vow to live fully in each moment and look at beings with eyes of compassion."*

Here is some advice on **how to start your day off better** by simplifying your routine as well, allowing for some time for mindful calm:

- Prepare your breakfast the night before.
- Lay out your outfit in advance.
- Avoid hitting the snooze button.
- Let sunshine brighten up your day.
- Clear off your bathroom counter.
- Turn up the music.
- Set up a bathroom schedule.
- Wait until you've bathed, dressed, and groomed before turning on your phone.

- Have a distraction-free breakfast.
- Dispense vitamins and medications into daily doses.
- Pack your lunch at dinnertime.
- Bring your hallway up to season.
- Store your bag and/or purse in the same location.
- Create a weather-ready area in your hallway.
- Make a checklist of must-have items.

Take some time to get yourself and your life organized to make for a much easier future. By having a calmer morning, and having a mindful cup of tea or coffee, or perhaps breakfast, will set you up for a happier existence.

Mindfulness in Relationships and Communication

68. MINDFUL RELATIONSHIPS

Mindfulness is a great tool for strengthening relationships. Whether this be a romantic relationship, one with a family member, or even friends. People who practice mindfulness regularly find their bonds with people much more solid for many reasons. They are more present when with the other person, listening better and engaging more. They also find it easier to regulate their emotions and to react in a calmer more considered manner to things, meaning things don't explode for no real reason. They are also more empathetic and open.

If this is something that you would like to work on, here is an exercise for you:

- Be present and pay attention. Focus only on the other person when they are with you. Concentrate on their words and features on their face. If your mind wanders, bring it back to that person.

- Practice acceptance and appreciation. Not everyone will act and behave in the way that you think they should, but that isn't a cause for an emotional reaction. Breathe mindfully and remind yourself to accept them and appreciate their wonderful points.

- Do mindful activities together, building your bond.

69. NOTICE BODY LANGUAGE

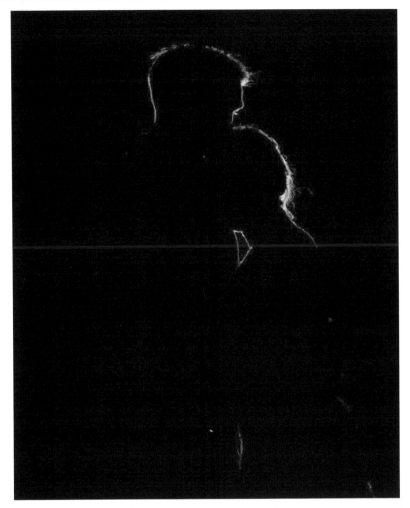

It's no secret that people don't often say what they really mean and that they keep their real thoughts inside. Think of all the times that you have plastered a fake smile on your face and pretended that everything was okay when really it wasn't, just to keep the peace.

By taking some time to notice body language, not only are you anchoring yourself in the present moment, but it will also assist you in being a better communicator, more emotionally intelligent, and more open and positive to others.

Here are **some questions to ask yourself while communicating with another person**, to ensure that you are giving out the right non-verbal cues and reading them correctly too:

- Are you aware that you are encoding a non-verbal message?
- Is the message being decoded the way you intended?
- Am I picking up the non-verbal cues of the party(s)?
- Am I doing it accurately?
- If yes to either of those, what do I do next?

This can help you to communicate in the most effective way possible.

70. LOVING KINDNESS

Loving kindness boosts compassion, helping you to look after yourself and other people. The mantra behind the meditation is *'May I be happy, may I be well, may I be filled with kindness and peace,'* which is something that we could all use a little more of. Mindfulness is a form of self-care, and it can lend itself to areas that we really need to work on. **If you are far too hard on yourself**, then a loving kindness meditation, such as this one, will really help you:

- Take a comfortable upright position, but relaxed.

- Start breathing mindfully, feel your breath moving in and out of your lungs, your body.

- Rest your hands comfortably in your lap. Close your eyes. Focus your awareness on your breath, your body. How does it feel right now? Notice these sensations, any feelings moving through your body while you breathe deeply.

- Think about loving kindness, how showing compassion to yourself is like the compassion you give others. Open yourself up to the goodness you extend to others. Remember a specific time you treated someone with loving kindness. When you put someone else's needs ahead of yours or when you did a good deed. What emotions did that generosity make you feel?

- Inhale and exhale slowly. Sit with the awareness of this feeling. Allow it to surround you, wash through you, touch all of your insides.

- Use your favorite affirmation to send yourself loving kindness. Repeat these words as often as you need. Focus on those words, that affirmation until you feel its message all through your body.

- Visualize someone important in your life and open the circle of loving kindness. This could even be a person who once brought you any kind of comfort or joy. Send them these feelings of loving kindness with affirmations.

- Next, visualize a "neutral" person. This could be a person you see often but do not know personally. Now, send them these feelings of loving kindness with affirmations.

- Then, think of someone who brings you challenges; it might be a person you wouldn't think to have compassion for. Let go of that anger, that resentment, and try sending them feelings of loving kindness with affirmations.

- Focus on spreading this out to everyone. Strangers, friends and loved ones, yourself, and even those you feel neutral for or feel negativity for. Intentionally extend this loving kindness as far as possible with your affirmations.

- Close the practice and focus on the feelings it generated. Did it boost your mood, your feelings about others and yourself? Remember this exercise the next time you start to have negative feelings not only about yourself, but in general.

Mindfulness in Body Exercises

71. BODY SCAN

The body scan is a very useful exercise when it comes to connecting with yourself and noticing what's going on. Although this is something that everyone can benefit from, because getting to know how you feel normally a lot better can assist you in noting when something might be wrong, it's highly recommended for those with chronic conditions.

It's amazing how little we know our bodies, how we go through life barely paying any attention because we have so much else to do. But our bodies are so important to us. It's vital that we treat them well. Checking in with our bodies ensures that we also get a sense of calm and connection with it, assisting us with our physical well-being.

This practice can involve a very narrow focus on specific parts of the body, and also involves an awareness of the body as a whole.

Here is **a good exercise that only takes five minutes or less** to get you started:

- Bring your attention to your body. Try closing your eyes if that helps. Notice the position your body is in. Feel the whole weight of your body, each of your limbs.
- Start with your mindful breathing.

- As you inhale deeply, visualize the oxygen waking up your body. When you let your breath out, notice the sensation of deep relaxation.

- Focus on your feet resting against the floor. The weight of your legs, the pressure of your feet at rest, vibrations coming through or across the floor, the temperature of the floor beneath your feet.

- Then, expand your focus to your entire body. Notice how your legs rest against the chair; your back and how it rests against the chair's back; your stomach and if it is tense. Relax these muscles if they are, then take a breath.

- Continue expanding your focus. Think about your hands, your arms, your shoulders, your throat and neck, your jaw, and your face. Are these muscles tense? If so, let them relax.

- Then, do a mindful check-in or body scan. Take a deep, cleansing breath. Turn your awareness to your whole body. Take another deep, cleansing breath. When you feel ready, slowly open your eyes.

72. MINDFUL WALKING

Walking is something that we do pretty much every day. Whether it's walking to work or to the shops, or even on your lunch hour, there should be at least five minutes of walking in your day in which you can integrate mindfulness. While walking, we're usually off somewhere else in our mind, planning or worrying, thinking about anything other than what we're doing right now. This can make walking very unpleasant, which is a shame. It doesn't have to be.

By walking mindfully, and enjoying the moment and the world around you, it can actually be a calming, lovely experience. Especially if you take this walk in nature.

Here is **a good exercise to help you start this**:

- Start by walking at a comfortable pace and resting your hands in a comfortable position.
  - o It can help you focus to count steps, for example, up to ten. In a small space? When you get to the tenth step, stop and use that moment to start over at one. You could even turn around or start a new walking path.
  - o Focus on how your foot rises and falls. Focus on the movement of your legs, your entire body. Take note of any body movement or shifting from side to side.
  - o Should anything else get your attention, gently bring it back to the mindful walking. It's natural for your mind to wander. Especially if you are walking outside. Try to get a sense of

your environment, staying safe, while focusing on the mindful walking.

- Bring your attention to the sounds in your environment. Simply pay attention without giving them a name or judging.

- Bring your attention to the aromas in your environment. Just take note. Don't try to judge or identify them.

- Bring your attention to what you see: objects, colors, and anything else.

- Remember to gently bring your attention back when something else gets your attention. Maintain a comfortable pace, not too fast or slow, and keep that level of awareness.

- As you finish your walk, return your awareness to the act of walking. Focus on your feet moving against the ground. Focus on how your body moves with every step.

73. MINDFUL EXERCISE

If exercise is something that you do regularly, it can be a fantastic trigger to ensure that you remember to incorporate mindfulness into your life. Working out mindfully actually helps you to have a better exercising experience anyway and can ensure that you get the most out of what you're doing. You will notice the sensations in your body more, helping you know what works best for you. Your breathing will be much more beneficial, and you'll also find it a lot simpler to keep to your targets.

Exercise is a time for you anyway, so **make it a real moment for you by just living in the moment**:

- Pause before your workout and remember what you're doing it for. Keeping your goal in mind can help you to keep going even if you don't feel like you want to. Start with some mindful breathing to help anchor you.

- Unplug. While it can be fun to listen to music as you exercise, it doesn't assist you in being mindful. Try going without music, to be able to listen to your body.

- Feel your body. Notice the sensations and how you feel before the exercise begins, notice the same throughout the exercise, and what's different, then do the same afterwards as well to see what's new. Do this with kindness and without judgement.

- Notice your breath and use it as a cue to try harder or slow down.

- Pay attention to your surroundings as well as your body. Use all five senses to make sure that you are feeling every aspect of the moment. Be aware of everything.

74. MOVEMENT

Movement can be the day to day things, such as walking around your house, heading up the stairs, and stretching up to reach something off the top shelf, or it can be an exercise like tai chi. Whatever it is, doing it mindfully for at least five minutes per day will make the experience much more enriching and will also remind you of the importance of moving. Our bodies are made to move, and it releases endorphins to make you feel good when you do, so really feeling that is very positive.

Here are **some tips to get the most out of your movement**:

- Know your intention for this movement, even if it's just to feel good. Keep this intention in mind for the five minutes of movement.

- Breathe, feel the breath travel through your body, gently caressing your muscles as it goes.

- Notice how your body feels with every different element of the movement.

- Notice your surroundings as well, the space around you, any sounds or sights.

- Notice how you feel once the five minutes have passed.

75. STRETCH

When sitting at a desk all day, we don't stretch enough. We get comfortable in our position of bad posture and narrowed eyes, while we stare at the screen and work on autopilot. Remembering to take a minute every so often to stretch our bodies can be beneficial to our physical health as well as our mental health. Having a moment for just us is what we need to get through the day and feel much better at the end of it. If you stretch and move your body, you won't return home feeling quite so bad.

While doing these stretches, breathe deep and notice the feeling in your chest. Also, notice the way that your body feels before the stretch, during it, and afterwards.

Here are **some desk stretches that you can do to take a moment from your work**:

Seated rotations

- Fold arms across your chest to grip shoulders.
- Twist upper body at your waist.
- Turn gently, as far as possible, from one side to the other.
- This stretches your lower back.

Shoulder stretches

- Hold one arm across your chest.
- Use other arm to press your elbow close to your chest.
- Repeat with other arm.

- This stretches your shoulders.

Slow shrug

- Gently raise shoulders toward your ears.
- Hold the stretch for a couple of seconds.
- Slowly let them rest.
- This releases the tension in your shoulders.

Back extension

- Straighten your back.
- Place your feet together on the floor.
- Press your palms against your lower back.
- Stretch your lower back by leaning against your hands.

Neck stretch

- Lift your chin away from your chest.
- Slowly turn your head, from one side to the other.
- Try to turn it as far as possible.
- This stretches out each side of your neck.

Single shoulder and neck extension

- Place one hand under your thigh.
- Tilt your head in the opposite direction of that hand.
- Then, tilt your chin towards your chest.
- This stretches out your neck and shoulder.
- Repeat with the other hand.

Backward shoulder stretch

- Stretch your arms behind your back as you stand up.
- Clasp your hands, then raise your clasped hands.
- This eases pressure for your back and shoulders.

Double shoulder stretch

- Raise both of your arms above your head.
- Turn your hands so your palms face the ceiling.
- Reach, from your shoulders, as close to the ceiling as possible.

- This stretches your shoulders.

Here is **another overall body stretch** for you:

- Stand with feet close together. Roll your neck first in one direction and then in the other.
- Raise your shoulders up to your ears and relax while lowering shoulders.
- Squeeze shoulder blades together and relax.
- Raise arms above head with thumbs hooked together breathing in and out through your stomach.
- Drop both arms to your sides, fingers pointing to your toes, stretching your back, without forcing.
- Straight arms, fingers pointing to the ceiling.
- Stand and lean your body to the left slowly to stretch the right side and vice-versa.
- Lie on your back, with feet close together, lift both feet off the ground, and hold for a few seconds. Lie on your back, bend your knees, place arms around your shins, and lift your knees and head.
- Do above exercise using one leg and then the other.
- Lie on your stomach and lift one straight leg off the ground and then the other leg.
- Stand straight and put your arms straight out ahead and bend your knees.
- Arms straight up in the air and lower slowly until hanging down with fingers pointing to the ground. Allow your body to hang for several seconds.

And if this is something that really interests you, Berkeley has a guide for you (*uhs.berkeley.edu/sites/default/files/wellness-mindfulstretchingguide.pdf*).

76. MASSAGE

Massage can be something that you do for yourself, for five minutes on a certain area of the body, to get rid of the tension in your body, or it can be something that you hire someone else to do to make your body feel better and less stressed. Either way, it's easy to make this experience a mindful one. There are so many body sensations involved to anchor yourself, and it also brings up emotions and thoughts. But rather than getting caught up in these feelings, simply observe them and let them pass.

Here are some tips for you:

- As you commence the massage, notice the first feeling arising inside you. Label it as talk, body, or image. Observe the rise and fall of this feeling.

- Notice as another feeling arises. Just as you just did before, label this new one as talk, body, or image. If more than one feeling arises at the same time, note them both as best you can.

- If you fall behind with your labeling, you need not try to catch up. Just stop where you are, take a deep breath, and wait for the next feeling to present itself. (It will get easier to keep up with labeling as you gain practice.)

- Don't feel frustrated if you cannot follow everything perfectly. Just neutrally observe and label: talk, body, or image. Singly, in tandem, or all at once. Allow everything to rise and fade away like clouds in an open sky.

- Continue in this way for as long as you like or until you complete the massage.

77. CLENCH YOUR FIST

This is a good mindfulness exercise to help you when you're dealing with difficult emotions, particularly when you are in a situation where you cannot let these feelings out. It's something that you can do under your desk, out of sight, to ground yourself if you're facing a challenge at work. By concentrating on the sensations in your hands, it can assist you in detaching from the emotion so **you can observe it properly and make a wise choice** about what you want to do next:

- Hold your hands so your thumbs and fingers point down.

- Make tight fists.

- Turn your fist over and release your fingers as you breathe mindfully.

- Focus on how you feel as that happens.

- Your hand will feel different when it's clenched and when it isn't. Just consider this for a few moments, repeating the exercise if necessary.

78. TENSE AND RELAX

Your muscles do a lot of work in your body without you even noticing, which is why they often ache and suffer stiffness and tension. Paying more attention to your muscles and making a mindful check-in with them can help relax them and make you use them better.

This exercise helps you to focus on all of your muscles and really pay attention to how they're feeling right now, while also relaxing you at the same time. It's a **great one for getting over stress and tension**:

- Start with a mindful check-in with your body. Then, perform mindful breathing, where one whole breath is inhaling from the tips of your toes to the very top of your head and exhaling right back down to your feet. Focus your awareness on what you're feeling in your body during these breath cycles (breathing in, then out is one breath cycle).

- Be sure to keep breathing deeply. Begin this exercise with your head. Flexing and relaxing the muscles of your face. For instance, raise your eyebrows. Focus on the muscle contraction. Hold this contraction for as long as you inhale without pain. As you exhale, drop your eyebrows to rest. Think about how different that muscle feels now that it's relaxed versus when it's tensed. Breathe through two more cycles.

- Now squeeze your eyelids shut. Hold this muscle contraction for one breath cycle. Relax. As you breathe mindfully through two more breath cycles, notice the sensations in your eyes being relaxed versus being squeezed shut.

- Now open your mouth really wide. Hold this muscle contraction while you inhale. Relax the muscle as you exhale. Concentrate on how your relaxed jaw feels through two more breath cycles.

- Now raise your shoulders up toward your earlobes. Then relax. Visualize your breath moving through your body, aiming toward your shoulders. Exhaling releases any tension. Think about how your shoulders feel as they are relaxed versus when the muscles are tight. Concentrate on the sensations in your shoulders through two more breath cycles.

- Raise both arms to shoulder height, then clench your hands tightly. Feel the tension in both of your arms – just your hands and arms, not your jaw or shoulders. Inhale as you tighten your muscles, and exhale as you relax your arms. Hold this muscle contraction through two breath cycles. Visualize your breath moving through your body, into the hand and arm muscles, then pulling the tension out as you exhale.

- Repeat the previous step focusing just on your hands, dropping them to your sides – so you don't tense up your arms instead.

Tightening your fists as you inhale and relaxing your hands as you exhale. Repeat through two breath cycles.

- Move to your chest, expand the muscles as wide as possible as you inhale. Focus on this feeling of tightness. Then exhale and release this tension. Then, as you breathe deeply, feel your stomach expand as you inhale. Notice the sensations in your chest as you breathe through two more breath cycles.

- Move down to your abdomen. Contract the muscles here so it feels like your belly button is trying to reach your spine. Hold this muscle contraction for as long as possible while you inhale slowly. As you exhale, visualize all the tension leaving your body. Repeat through two more breath cycles.

- Now move down to your buttocks. Squeeze the muscles and hold the tension as you inhale. Release all the tension as you exhale. Notice the sensations of tension and relaxation. Focus on these sensations through two more breath cycles.

- Now stretch your feet, pointing your toes upward toward the ceiling. Focusing on your feet and leg muscles. Notice the tense feeling in your thighs and lower legs. Hold that muscle contraction and think about how that feels. Exhale and let all that tension go. Repeat through two more breath cycles.

- Then, focus on your toes. Curl them, tensing up those muscles as you inhale. Relax as you exhale. Think about that sensation in your toes through two more breath cycles.

- Complete the exercise with a mindful check-in. Inhale and exhale through two breath cycles as you focus on any remaining tension in your body. Send your breath to those areas and release the tension as you exhale. When you feel ready, open your eyes. Slowly move your body. Roll into a comfortable seated position, if you started on the floor, or stand up very slowly from your seated position.

79. GET UNCOMFORTABLE

This might sound strange, since most of the other exercises have told you to get comfortable before starting your practice, but what will get you more in touch with your bodily sensations than being uncomfortable? Stretching yourself into a position that you don't usually take, and noticing how this makes your body feel, will assist you in really zoning in on the present moment. This might not be something that you can keep up for five whole minutes, but it doesn't have to be. You can alternate it between thirty seconds of discomfort and thirty seconds of comfort, so you can notice the changes in your body.

Here is **an exercise to get started with**, introducing just a mild discomfort in your body to see how this makes you feel. That way, you can see if it works for you:

- Run your hands and fingers along the length of your legs. Feeling as much of these limbs as you can, touching the softer and harder parts across your muscles and skin. Take five breaths and experience how it really feels to spend time with a part of your body that you usually ignore.

- Really notice your legs. Examine every detail, every part you haven't really noticed before. Think about how many journeys you have taken together, how far they have brought you. Acknowledge their power and strength.

- Soften your gaze; allow your eyes to close.

- Slowly stretch your body forward to feel the tension and sensations in your legs. Anything beyond some mild discomfort isn't good.

- Select three words to describe how you feel as you hold this stretch.

- Shift your hands to where the stretch is most intense along your leg. Move your fingers along that taut muscle.

- As you do this, imagine your breath drifting in and out of your body while you take five mindful breaths.

- Release your stretch and stand up. Take another five mindful breaths.

- Resume your stretch, then take another five mindful breaths.

- Repeat this stretching process until you are ready.

- Release your final stretch, then take five final mindful breaths.

Mindful Moods and Emotions

80. MINDFUL APPRECIATION

Gratitude often takes a back seat when times are hard. When you're busy and stressed, it's hard to recall all of the things that you should be grateful for, but there is always something. Even during the most difficult periods of our lives, if we look hard enough, we can find something that we are thankful for. The fact that we are alive and breathing, for one!

Practicing this every single day can actually help to rewire your brain, to bring out a much more positive outlook, which, of course, will be useful for the future. This **gratitude can help your well-being and overall health**, and it only takes five minutes:

- Start, as always, with mindful breathing and some mindful observation to bring yourself into the present moment.

- Once your mind is calm, think of ten things that you are grateful for that you wouldn't normally take the time to appreciate. If this is hard, think very small, think about the more intricate details of things, consider the people in your life who are a blessing right now.

- If you still have time, consider how these ten things make your life better, how they all play into one another, and do this with a faint smile playing on your lips.

- Think about these things even after you have finished the exercise to remind yourself that you have something to be happy about. If you do this every day for a week, you will have seventy things to be grateful for already.

81. SELF-COMPASSION PAUSE

We often have far more compassion for others than we do for ourselves. The things that we have negativity about or that we punish ourselves for are things that we would tell others aren't a big deal or shouldn't be worried about. This self-punishment is very unhealthy and can actually lead to a terrible negative cycle that's hard to get out of.

Treating ourselves badly becomes a habit, and sometimes, we don't even realize that it's happening. That's why we all need a self-compassion pause from time to time, to take care of ourselves and to remind ourselves that we aren't as bad as we might think.

Here is **a great exercise for this**:

- Ground yourself with a five-minute pause.

- Place your hand on your heart, touch the center of your chest, or give yourself a hug, then take a few mindful breaths. It could be helpful to try this with your eyes closed.

- Embrace your pain. Think of what you might say to a family member, friend, or loved one if they were experiencing this pain, then say that to yourself.

- Use a declarative statement, such as *"I am suffering," "This is painful,"* or *"Suffering is human,"* to help yourself embrace this pain.

- Then, use a declarative statement, such as *"I can love and accept myself as I am," "I am open to my experience as it is,"* or *"I can experience love and kindness,"* to give yourself some compassion.

- Go back to your daily life, with an intentional mind-set to give yourself acceptance and compassion.

82. SELF-INQUIRY

Self-inquiry is about checking in with yourself to get to know me. This might sound silly, like something you don't need to do, but giving it a go can make you realize that, because you've been living on autopilot for such a long time, you don't actually feel like yourself right now. By discovering this, you can then go on to fix it.

Here is a good **five-minute exercise to get you started with getting to know you:**

- Sit quietly with your eyes closed, focusing on the sensation of breathing. The air going in and out through your nose and mouth, your chest rising and falling, your belly expanding and deflating.

- After a few deep breaths, ask yourself, *"Who am I?"* Do not try to answer this question, simply allow it to ripple through you.

- Once your mind is calm again, ask yourself, *"Who is thinking this thought?"*

- Recognize that, at some level, the word *I* reflects something much deeper.

- For the practice of self-inquiry to work its magic, you must recognize at some level that the word 'I,' though superficially referring to the body and mind, actually points to something much deeper.

- After a couple more moments, ask yourself again, *"Who am I?"* The answer might not present itself, but if it does, it will be more in a vibrant feeling than a thought.

83. OBSERVING THOUGHTS

The point of mindfulness is not to block your thoughts out; it's about just observing them and letting them go. Let them slide past you without giving them too much attention and without getting caught up in them. These thoughts can be positive or negative; they can be emotional, personal, or nothing in particular. The trick is to not judge them, to just let them go by.

Here is **an exercise that is wonderful for this**:

- Get into a comfortable position. Then, rest your eyes on one spot or close them.

- Imagine yourself in a peaceful place, such as next to a gently flowing brook where leaves can float along its surface. Pause for a count of ten.

- Then, visualize each of your thoughts resting on one of those leaves. Allow them to pass you by. Do this with each thought, even the happy thoughts.

- Should your thoughts come to a stop, keep your focus on the brook. Pause for a count of twenty.

- Watch the brook flow, keeping its pace. Letting your thoughts just float along. Don't try to push the brook along or "get rid" of your feelings. Simply allow them to float along by you.

- Place every thought on a leaf, positive, negative, doubting; just let them float. Pause for another count of twenty.

- If a thought sticks around, allow it until it's ready to pass by. That thought may come back around, just watch it pass by again. Pause for another count of twenty.

- Acknowledge a painful or difficult feeling if it arises by saying, *"I am feeling..."* Rest those thoughts on their own leaves, too, then let them pass right on by.

- It is normal for your thoughts to distract you and keep you from being totally present. Just bring your focus back to the brook and its leaves when you recognize that you are sidetracked.

84. DISSIPATE ANGER

Anger is one of the strongest emotions, and when it flares up, it can be hard to think of mindfulness as an answer. When you're at the end of your fuse and all you want to do is let this rage out, getting calm might feel like something impossible. But that simply makes the exercise even more important, because nothing good is achieved when acting with a hot head. Calming down and stepping out of this emotion to distance yourself is the best way to make smart choices.

Here is a great exercise **to help cool down that burning hot rage** by just experiencing it fully and accepting it:

- Go to a quiet, distraction-free space where you can stand comfortably. Focus on mindful breathing, taking some deep breaths.

- After grounding yourself, place your feet a short distance apart, hip width apart. Dig in your heels, bend your knees for support, and concentrate on balance and the floor's stability. Roll your shoulders back.

- Notice the sensations moving within your body. If body parts are filled with tension, now is a great time to massage away that tension.

- Recall the incident that brought up these uncomfortable feelings. Let these emotions come to the surface.

- Speak these feelings out loud, using an *"I am…"* statement. Repeat it, as loudly or as quietly, as quickly or as slowly, as often as you need to, to really feel that emotion.

- Take note of the sensations moving within your body. Observe them, then name them to separate yourself from its instability.

- If there are other feelings, speak them out loud as well, using an *"I am…"* statement.

- After you have stated all of your feelings, relax your body and take several mindful breaths.

- Writing these emotions down after the fact can help you free yourself.

85. SORTING EMOTIONS, SENSATIONS, THOUGHTS

Sorting through your emotions, sensations, and thoughts can be a great way to untangle the mess inside your brain, which has wormed its way into your body as well, and to return to the present moment. Emotions can be harmful to our well-being if we get caught up in them and we allow them to rule us. Noticing them and detaching from them can help us to control the power that they have over us. The same with body sensations. Sometimes, just noting that tightness in your chest lessens the control it has over you.

With your thoughts, it's important to remember that they are just that. Thoughts. Nothing they say is necessarily true, particularly when you're being unkind to yourself.

Here is **a great exercise to help you with this**:

- Begin with mindful breathing.
- Focus on your emotions or feelings. Name these emotions, if you can do so easily; otherwise, just generate awareness of them.
- Where do these emotions occur in your body? Do the physical sensations drift, move, or shift?
- What do these emotions make you feel?
- What thoughts are you having with these emotions? Have awareness of them without judgment.
- Take a moment to sit with this new awareness – the movement of feelings, thoughts, and physical sensations within your body.
- Bring your focus back to your breathing.

86. GET THROUGH ANXIETY

Anxiety is a sensation of worry or fear or even just unease. It affects everyone at some point in their lives and can be mild or severe. If the anxiety comes when a stressful event is coming up, then it's unlikely to be something to seriously worry about, but if it becomes life-consuming, it's better to get some medical assistance for this condition. This can be caused by an imbalance of chemicals, trauma in your past, or an overactive brain.

Whatever level of anxiety you feel, mindfulness can help you with the symptoms of it, as shown by the exercise below:

- Choose a comfortable position. Make sure you feel secure, not straining. Loosen tight clothing and relax your body's muscles – chest, shoulders, and stomach. Close your eyes and notice your body's stillness.

- Focus on your breathing. Inhale deeply through the nose, bringing your breath all the way down into your diaphragm. Exhale slowly through your mouth. Repeat.

- Notice how calm you feel as you exhale. Breathe out stress and tension as your breathing finds a comfortable rhythm.

- Acknowledge the feelings or thoughts you're having. Some of these thoughts may be distressing. Remember, it's okay for your mind to wander; it's normal. Simply observe and don't judge these thoughts. If a specific feeling or thought holds your attention, take note of it and then bring your attention back to your breathing. Notice the thought or feeling, but then let it go.

- Imagine yourself in your favorite place – a garden, the beach, a mountain cabin, or anywhere that puts you at ease. Focus on the details of this place. The colors of the flowers or plants, the refreshing sea breeze blowing, or the sounds of the waves. Let these details relax you and continue focusing on your breathing. Stay calm, letting your feelings and thoughts move and change.

- Imagine a situation that brings you fear. Notice the discomfort this situation gives you. Let the discomfort be; don't resist it.

- Keep breathing and relax. Let that discomfort dissipate. Remember that acceptance will help you when you experience anxiety. Learn to welcome and accept these thoughts and feelings, and then let them float away.

- Hold on to moments of happiness as they occur during the day, grab hold of it, keep that feeling within your awareness. In those moments, count to fifteen, which allows your brain to establish new pathways. Use these pathways often, and the grooves will get deeper.

- Bring your focus slowly back to your breathing, when you feel you are ready. Then, focus on your body, then the surroundings. Move gently and stretch, as you open your eyes.

87. ADDICTION AWARENESS

One of the first things that we need to do when it comes to overcoming addiction is being aware of the cause of it. There's an unhappiness that has come from somewhere; whether this is trauma or depression, dissatisfaction or fear, there is something that you need to be aware of. Because of this, mindfulness is often used in addiction treatment with very positive results (as researched here: *www.ncbi.nlm.nih.gov/pmc/articles/PMC5907295/*.

Practicing mindfulness can also help those with addiction identify the chaos in our lives, sort through any negativity that can lead to these issues, and help to identify boundaries.

Here is **a great exercise to try to start with when it comes to addiction issues**:

- Focus on taking mindful, deep breaths.

- Notice the sensations of the changes in your breathing, and the gentle rhythm it is creating within you. "Letting it be, just as it is." Each inhale and exhale announcing the next.

- Expand your awareness to the sensations of your body. Sitting upright and with dignity – bring your attention to the surface beneath you and the support it provides. Root your body into its strength and become aware of your connection to it – complete, whole, and in this moment, you are grounded by its unwavering resolve.

- As you sit there, visualize a grand mountain, whose peaks pierce smoky clouds and continue upward where the air is clear and the view is endless. A mountain with slopes that are both jagged and gentle; supported by a vast foundation, rooted deep in the bedrock of the earth. This mountain is a monument to all that is solid, grand, unmoving, and beautiful.

- Are there trees? Does snow blanket its lofty heights? Perhaps waterfalls cascading as mist into an open sky?

- However it is – let it be as it is: a perfect creation.

- Be this mountain, and share in its stillness.

- Grounded in your posture, your head its skyward peak, supported by the rest of your form, granting you an awe-inspiring perspective of the landscape before you, behind you, and about you, which flows from your center into the distance horizon.

- Be this mountain.

- And take on its stability as your own. From the top of your crown, down your neck, and into the balance of your shoulders, like cliffs, descending into your arms and forearms, and coming to rest in the valley of your hands.

- Be the mountain.

- Your feet, legs, and hips, its base – solid and rooted beneath you – a foundation, extending up your spine and abdomen: a core of stability.

- The rhythm of your breath is all that moves you. A living mountain: alive and aware, "yet unwavering in inner stillness: completely what you are, beyond words and thought: a centered, grounded, unmovable presence."

- A mountain, which witnesses the sun travel through the sky, glowing, casting shadows and colors across the landscape beneath it. As each moment passes, on the surface of the mountain's stillness, life and activity bloom: snows melt, streams run down its face, trees and flowers bloom and die and bloom again as the wildlife returns and departs with the seasons.

- Be the mountain, who will be called beautiful and inspiring, and dark and ominous, and knows that it is all of those things and less.

- Be the mountain – which sits and sees how night follows day and back again. Which knows the sun by the warmth it brings on rising, and the stars by the way they show in a darkened sky.

- Through it all, the mountain sits. Aware of the changes that each moment brings, around it and to it. Yet, it stays true to itself. Still, while seasons flow from one to another, as air currents swirl from hot and cold, and the weather turns from tame to turbulent. Some so treacherous as to tear at its surface.

- Still – none of this concerns the mountain, whose serenity is housed within, and cannot be disturbed by fleeting furor.

- "In the same way, as you sit in meditation, you can learn to experience the mountain as a means to embody the same centered, unwavering stillness and groundedness in the face of all that changes in your life – over seconds, and hours, and years."

- Like the mountain, you will feel the nature of your body and mind shift as the nature of the world around you shifts. You will have periods varying in intensity – of darkness and light, of activity and inactivity, and moments that fill your life with color.

- Through it all, be the mountain, and call on its patient strength and stability within you. Let it empower you to encounter each moment with mindful composure and compassionate clarity.

88. MINDFUL GRATITUDE

Gratitude is a much better way to live your life. Being grateful and happy for what you have leads to a much more positive outlook, which, of course, will keep you happier and healthier. It's been proven that gratitude makes you live longer, feel better, and improves your social life. When you're caught up in thoughts, particularly negative ones, it can be hard to practice this, which is why you need five minutes of gratitude each day.

There are a number of ways in which you can practice this in a very simple way, such as **these three short exercises**:

- Find a place where you can walk slowly and intently. With each step, think of something or someone that you're thankful for.

- Focus on how you say 'thank you' throughout the day. Is it simply a habitual response, a lame afterthought, nearly forgotten? How do you feel as you express gratitude, even for minor transactions? Absentminded, pressured, even stressed? Take a moment for a mindful check-in. Have you already moved on to the next exchange, mentally, physically?

- Each day, as you reach a moment to say "thanks," take one moment for a mindful check-in. Try to identify what you are saying 'thank you' for. Is there something beyond what's being exchanged? When you can identify it, take that moment to say an aware and mindful 'thank you.'

89. TAKE CONTROL

People who practice mindfulness regularly feel much more in control of themselves and their lives. There is something a little chaotic about living on autopilot, never grounding yourself, which is why it's so important to take five minutes to remind yourself of the right now. Learning to observe our thoughts and sensations, letting go when necessary are skills that will completely transform our brains. Rewiring it where necessary.

Here is **an exercise to help at moments you feel particularly out of control**:

- Find a space where you can take five minutes, feeling safe and without distractions.

- Focus on mindful breathing. Notice the sensation of your breath moving in and out of your body.

- Acknowledge your emotion. Label it to take control over the emotion and help put distance between yourself and that feeling. *"I feel [labeled emotion] right now, and this feels [good, bad, etc.]."*

- Explore the roots of this emotion.

- Resist the urge push away negative feelings. Accept and allow yourself to feel it, instead.

- Focus on the parts of this situation that you can change, and try to accept what you cannot change. In some cases, the only thing you can change is your reaction.

- Stay aware of your breathing and use it to reconnect with the present moment. Staying aware of your five senses, and especially your breathing, can cool down heightened emotions and help you approach issues or events with calm and control.

90. AFFIRMATIONS

Using affirmations while you do mindful breathing can be a good way of centering yourself in the present moment in a positive way, reminding yourself that any negative thoughts are just that, and not the truth, and keeping you going on the right path.

As you focus on your breath, repeat the affirmation over and over. Here are **some suggestions for affirmations to start with**, but eventually, you will probably want to come up with one of your own:

- I always have guidance and protection.
- I create my own happiness.
- I bring love into my life.
- I create acceptance and love for myself.
- My life is going well.
- I bring prosperity into my life.
- My body is in good health.
- I take the necessary action.
- I contain the power of the Divine.
- I trust in Divine power.
- My heart is open to love.
- I create my future.

- I release my anger to the Universe.
- I give my fear to the Universe.
- The past is over and gone.
- In this moment, I am whole and perfect just as I am.
- My life starts today.
- I am worthy of achieving my dreams.
- I am good enough just as I am.
- People accept and love me.
- All things are possible.
- I persevere because I am strong.
- My choices make positive changes.
- I can achieve true balance.
- I follow the rhythm of life.
- My inner voice is trustworthy.
- I attract prosperity.
- My body is enough.
- I am filled with happiness.
- I am loved and free.
- I create new opportunities.
- I have gratitude for my magnificent life.
- I make the choices that create my path.
- I can find love.

91. LABEL YOUR EMOTIONS

Emotions have a way of getting the better of us, particularly the strong ones, such as anger or sadness. We are so used to letting them sweep over us and dictate how we behave that we forget these feelings aren't actually in the driving seat of our lives. We are, and by making sure that we don't allow these emotions to get the better of us, our reactions can always be much smarter and more considered.

Think about a time that you have let anger get the better of you and how you reacted. Now consider how you wish you had behaved with the benefit of hindsight. By labeling your emotions and noting them for what they are, rather than letting them control you, you get that benefit of detachment and hindsight right away. By taking this moment and having a pause, the way that you behave afterwards will be very different.

Here **you can see the difference:**

The domino effect of letting the emotions take control

- Event occurs...
- Body stiffens, clenches...
- "I can't believe this!" / "They are so wrong!" / "This shouldn't be!"
- "I am angry / sad / frustrated / humiliated / etc."
- Body stiffens, clenches more...
- "I'm going to let them have it!"

See how this affects your whole body? Every part of you is consumed with the emotion, and it gets the better of you. It makes you want to blow up and react in a certain way.

Taking a mindful pause and labeling the emotion

- "My body is telling me I'm angry, sad, etc." (deep, slow breath in)

- "I'm having thoughts that this is upsetting." (slow exhale out)

- "Anger... anger... anger..." (deep, slow breath in)

- Body slows down. (slow exhale out)

- "Sad... sad... sad..." (deep, slow breath in)

- What do you notice?

By labeling the emotion as soon as you feel any alert to it swelling up, and recognizing it as just an emotion rather than your truth, you get a moment to cool down, distance yourself, and think how you would like to behave.

It might sound a little strange but give it a try next time a strong emotion rears its ugly head. See how it makes a difference.

92. RAIN

RAIN is an exercise invented by *Doctor Goldstein* to help you take a pause, particularly when a strong emotion is around. It's a little like labeling emotions but goes a little deeper into really exploring how you're feeling. This practice is good for helping to really sort out why you're feeling certain things and what effect that's having on you. These emotions might not be positive or helpful, so by separating yourself, you can decide whether you want to give yourself over to them or not.

Goldstein describes it as: *"Seeing a movie, standing back and watching the actors play out their dramas, by non-identifying with your story and seeing it as impermanent, this will help assist in loosening your own tight grip of identification."*

- "R" is to recognize when a strong emotion is present.
- "A" is to allow or acknowledge that it is indeed there.
- "I" is to investigate and bring self-inquiry to the body, feelings, and mind.
- "N" is to non-identify with what's there.

As Goldstein describes it: *"Turning into our emotions can feel a bit foreign since most of us live in such a pain denying culture. Isn't it time to begin acknowledging stress, anxiety or pain rather than suppressing, repressing, or all-too-quickly medicating it? Can we learn to view these challenges as a rite of passage instead of running away from them?"*

93. ABC

ABCs is a mindful exercise that helps you to sort through any difficult emotions and to harness this awareness to ensure that you move forward in a positive manner. It's great to **label your feelings** and to recognize them for what they are, but sometimes, you need a little more **to decide how you're going to move forward** in the right way for you:

- **A**: *Awareness*. Take a mindful moment with some breathing, anchor yourself, and work out how you're feeling right now. What your emotions are, how your body feels, what thoughts are running through your head. Cultivate this awareness as a springboard for the next part.

- **B**: *Breathe* and *balance*. While sorting through these emotions, it can be hard to remain detached, but that's what you need to do to ensure that you move forward correctly. Keep mindfully breathing until the sense of balance comes.

- **C**: *Compassionate choices*. Now that you have dug deep to feel your emotions, be compassionate with yourself and use kindness as you make your next choice. Doing nothing is an option, especially when heavy emotions are involved, so don't forget about that.

- **S**: *Support*. If you need the help of others, never be afraid to ask for it.

94. WORRY TIME

Scheduling time to worry might seem like a ridiculous idea, but if anxiety is something that you feel is controlling you and your life, then it might be something to consider. This doesn't mean taking five minutes every single day to worry, because that will only spiral and make you feel much worse.

No, instead, this is choosing the time to worry about something when you can actually do something about it. When you start to notice this, you realize that most of your worrying is done about something that you have no control over *right now*.

'Oh, I have so much to do tomorrow morning...' right as you're going to bed.

'I'm so worried that I will be late to work...' as you wait for the bus.

'I'm scared that my mom is unhappy at the moment.'

When those worries crop up, you need to remind yourself that there is nothing you can do about that at the moment. You need to sleep, so you can't check everything off your 'to do' list at night. You can't control when the bus arrives. You also don't have any power over your mother's emotions. Worrying about these things when you can't do anything about them only hurts you and really damages your ability to do anything effective about it.

Oh, I have so much to do tomorrow morning...but I can't do anything about that right now, so I will worry about it at 7:00 a.m. tomorrow when I can make a plan.'

'I'm so worried that I will be late to work...but worrying won't change that, so I will worry about it at 9:00 a.m. when I'm either at work on time, or not, but I can call in and let them know.'

'I'm scared that my mom is unhappy at the moment...but I can't help her at this moment. I will worry about it this evening at 6:00 p.m. when I can call her and check in.'

Then you need to connect to the present moment, take five minutes of mindfulness, to connect with what you can do right now. You can't change the past or the future, only what's happening this second.

Here is a list of **grounding exercises that you can use to pull yourself away from that worry** until you can do something about it:

- Take a moment to remember who you are; out loud, speak your name, your birthday, what you did today, where you stand, and what you plan to do next.

- Focus on taking ten mindful breaths. Count them if it helps, assigning a number each time you breathe out.

- Use something cold to draw your attention. Try splashing cold water on your face or hold a cold beverage between your hands. Concentrate on this sensation. Take note of the wet condensation on the outside of the can or the softness of the towel against your face as you dry it off.

- Have you woken up in the middle of the night? Look around the room to remind yourself where you are. Feel the blankets and bed around you. Remind yourself of who you are, what year it is, how old you are, and any familiar sounds you can hear.

- Are you with other people? If you feel comfortable doing so, concentrate very closely on what they say and do. Take mindful breaths, then remind yourself what you are doing with them.

- Are you sitting in a meeting or at a restaurant? Recognize the chair you're sitting on, the weight of your entire body resting against it. Focus on the sensation of the chair, its arms, its back, its legs against your arms, legs, and back.

- No matter where you are, you can always simply stop and listen. Focus on and identify the sounds you can hear. Slowly shift your focus to distant sounds.

- Press the soles of your feet into the ground. Concentrate on the sensation as the weight of your body impacts the ground.

- Clench your hands into fists or clap your palms against the sides of your thighs. Feel the muscles tighten in your arms or focus on the noise your hands make. Concentrate on the sensations that are generated.

- Flick an elastic band that you can wear comfortably on your wrist. Focus on the sensation as you feel it spring back against your skin.

- Can you take a moment to step outside? Be mindful of the environment by concentrating on the temperature, if the wind is blowing, if you can smell any plants or flowers. Can you see trees or shrubbery? Notice the shape and color of these plants.

- Do you have a pet? Take a moment to play with them. Pet its fur, scratch its scales, or rub your finger over its feathers. Is the skin scaly, slimy? Does its body have bright colors as it swims in its bowl? How or what does it eat?

- Pick up a pillow, piece of clothing, or other interesting fabric and take a moment to touch it. Think about how it feels. Focus on the sensation of touching it. Is it rough, smooth, soft, silky?

- Do you tend a garden or have indoor plants? Run your fingers through the soil, across the leaves, or simply talk to your plant.

95. Give Yourself Credit

You are doing a much better job than you think you are. Yes, really. The inner critic inside of you isn't speaking the truth; it's all just thoughts that don't really mean anything. But **if these negative thoughts continue to crop up no matter what**, then it could be time to try this practice:

- Recognize how harsh your inner critic is by considering how you would react to someone else saying the exact same things to you.

- Acknowledge these thoughts, then remember it is only a thought – temporary, not a fact, and not necessary to focus on.

- Use mindful breathing to inhale positivity and exhale negativity.

- Talk to yourself as though you are best friends.

96. TO BE

Instead of creating your 'to do' list every single day, why not have a go at thinking about your 'to be' list. Instead of worrying about what has to be done, consider what sort of person you want to be, what qualities you wish to have, what your goals are. Thinking about these mindfully will **put your 'to do' list into perspective**. Is everything that you're doing working towards your goals:

- Start with thinking about what you want. Is this a better career? More money? More friends? To fall in love?

- Now think about what qualities you should inhabit to make this happen. You might need to be more focused on your work, more actively ambitious, louder about your achievements so they are recognized. Or perhaps you need to try and be more outgoing, more sociable, kinder, and more loving.

- Now what do you need to do to make this happen? Get more organized? Go to classes? Accept invitations more?

Your 'to be' list might not always work out, and it may change constantly, so it's something that you must review every so often to confirm that you're still on the path you wish to be on.

97. MINDFUL JAR

A jar for mindfulness is an activity often suggested to do with children but can be just as effective for adults as well. It's a visual metaphor to help you when it comes to separating your thoughts, feelings, and behaviors. It can be particularly useful in the early days of coming to grips with mindfulness, and once it's been made you can always come back to it.

Here are some tips to make this work for you:

- Select a container you would like to fill with water and glitter. Choose three different colors of glitter to represent feelings, thoughts, and behaviors. Add preferred amounts of each color of glitter, then seal the container.

- What does this container of water and glitter mean?

- Think of this container as your mind, where the glitter represents how feelings, thoughts, and behaviors can mix.

- At first, our mind is calm. Where thoughts, feelings, and behaviors are at rest. Like the glitter at the bottom of the container.

- Then, something "shakes up" our mind. An argument, oversleeping, or some other kind of event occurs – move the container around to see how the glitter swirls in the water. If you think about a happy event – a birthday party, an unexpected visit from an old friend – and shake the container, notice how the swirling looks the same.

- Now with those thoughts, feelings, and behaviors swirling, we struggle to see clearly. Those emotions and desires are clouding our vision.

- If life is shaking us up, being still is one way to regain calm, to see clearly like we did before life "shook" us up. Consider that you cannot force the glitter to fall back to rest; you must wait for it to settle on its own.

- As you embrace stillness, take a moment to consider that the glitter does not disappear. It never will; even as it settles, it will remain at the bottom of "your mind." Your feelings, thoughts, and desires (or behaviors) are always there. But, when things become clear, your feelings are no long in control, no longer blocking what you need to see to make decisions and plan for what comes next.

- This new awareness is a kind of wisdom; allowing yourself to see things as they are – even when your feelings and thoughts threaten to cloud your vision – and making an active choice in how you respond or don't.

98. THOUGHTS AS OPINIONS

Thoughts are only opinions. Positive or negative, there isn't anything about thoughts that make them real. It might be our inner critic that everyone thinks we don't deserve our job (which there's no way you can know what *everyone* else really thinks), or that we're great at driving (says who?), or even that we feel a bit deflated today.

These are just thoughts, but we treat them as gospel, putting far too much trust in them. In reality, what we need to do is recognize these thoughts for what they are. Just thoughts, just an opinion. Something to observe, not get caught up in.

Once you start noting this, every time you have a thought you can detach from it, seeing it as something to just let pass you by. As soon as you stop getting caught up in your thoughts, allowing them to control you, the clearer your mind will be.

This might not seem easy at first, but here is **a way to detach from negative thoughts** every time they crop up in three simple steps:

- The negative thought crops up, usually after a trigger like something going wrong. *"I can't do anything right."*

- As soon as this thought crops up, catch yourself and think (or even say aloud to yourself to really anchor it): *"I think I can't do anything right."*

- Finally, you can change it to: *"I've noticed I have a thought that I can't do anything right."* Which really pulls you away from the thought and allows it to slide off you more easily.

99. THOUGHT DUMP

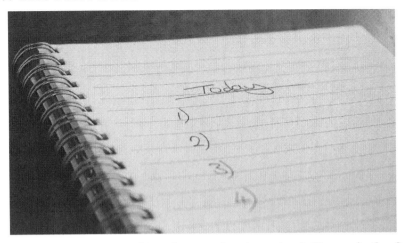

A thought dump is something that people who enjoy it like to do for five minutes in the morning. Writing without thinking, simply getting all their thoughts and emotions out, worries too. The act of writing it down can be cathartic and can also give the worries somewhere to be so they don't have to be in your mind anymore.

Tomorrow morning, wake up, or perhaps try it at the end of the day, whatever suits you best, and just write for five minutes without stopping. Whatever comes to mind, get it down. Notice how you feel before and after the exercise.

As you write, feel the pen in your hands, notice the sound it makes on the paper, consider how you feel – and to make it even more mindful, **try this exercise**:

- Get pen and paper.
- Sit somewhere quiet and relaxing.
- Take ten mindful breaths.
- Focus on the feelings and emotions in your mind.
- Begin to mindfully write about those emotions by describing them.
- Your emotions will change while you write. Follow your emotions. As they change, write about how they are changing.

100. EMBRACE EVERY THOUGHT AND EMOTION

As you have seen from a lot of exercises in this book, mindfulness isn't about ignoring thoughts and feelings, it's about observing and accepting them. You don't have to give weight to them, and it's better not to get caught up in them, but they are always going to be there. You can't go through life without difficulty, without anger or upset. You need to embrace it, accept it as a part of you, and find inner peace with it. Once you learn to work with these difficult emotions, they won't be able to control you anymore. You will have the power back once more.

Here is an exercise **to help you embrace everything that happens within you**:

- Acknowledge – after you notice what you are feeling, stop, take a mindful breath, and acknowledge it. Recognize each feeling, positive or negative, to help move past it easier.

- Name – identify the specific emotion you are feeling. Doing so will give you a sense of power in controlling it.

- Embrace – distance yourself from the instability of the emotion by embracing and accepting it. *"I feel [acknowledged emotion]. That is acceptable."*

- "This too shall pass" – every emotion is all right at some point, in some situation, so allow yourself to feel it, or they will linger. Allowing yourself to just feel that emotion helps it pass on, even if you can't or shouldn't act on it.

- Explore – after the height of the emotion has passed, explore the roots of that emotion.

- Respond – not all feelings require a physical act. Some can be acknowledged and processed simply by taking one moment to embrace it. This new awareness keeps you from responding in a reckless or irresponsible way.

5 EASY WAYS TO BE MINDFUL EVERY DAY

Once the thirty days are up and you have seen the benefits that mindfulness has brought to your life, chances are you will want to keep it up. Slipping back into that unconscious living is not the way you want to live your life anymore. But how do you make sure that you stick to it?

The good news is that the hard work is already done. You have started building the habit and shown yourself that you can make five minutes for yourself, however busy you are. You haven't been making excuses, so don't start to do so now.

Here are **some tips to help you:**

1. Set a reminder – make sure it's at a reasonable time every day to make sure you won't be busy and forget. In the morning or when

you get home from work could help.

2. Use the bells – many apps have the bells feature that will ring throughout the day, just reminding you that you need to take a moment to breathe and be present.

3. Introduce someone else to the practice – there's no better way to encourage yourself to do something than with other people, and while you teach someone else, the benefits will be remembered more clearly.

4. Combine it with a certain activity that you have to do every day so there's no way you can forget.

5. Breathe while you wait – there will always be something that you have to wait for, so always be sure to use that time to focus on your breath rather than allowing your brain to run at a million miles an hour.

CONCLUSION

"The present moment is filled with joy and happiness.
If you are attentive, you will see it."

– Thich Nhat Hanh

So, as this book has shown you, it's actually much easier to introduce mindfulness into your life than it first seems. Dragging yourself out of your unconscious mind and living in the present moment, even for only five minutes a day, will give you the endless health and well-being benefits talked about in the introduction: better sleep, a calmer life, a happier existence.

There are a number of ways to bring this practice into your life as well. You have discovered one hundred new and exciting ways throughout this book to get you started. Some which will work for you and others that you might not enjoy so much, but this is just the beginning. The resources chapter at the end of this book will give you some more places to start looking.

Eventually, you can even invent practices of your own to help you live in the present moment.

Once you have achieved a quieter mind, you will see how busy your thoughts were before, and how a lot of these thoughts were completely unnecessary, just a tangled mess that created a lot of stress that you didn't need. Now, you can move forward without this. You can live the life that you were always supposed to, enjoying each moment as it occurs rather than worrying about ones that have already been or ones that haven't come yet – ones that you cannot do anything about.

Enjoy your inner peace, and good luck for the future.